How to Make Insurance Work for you- Your Personal Finance Guide

David Okonah

DAO Publishing Company Limited

Dedication

To my incredible wife, Maureen, whose unwavering love and support have been my rock throughout this journey. Your belief in me has been a constant source of strength, and I am forever grateful for the partnership we share. Together, we've navigated the ups and downs of life, always finding a way to make the most of every moment. This book is as much yours as it is mine, for you have been my greatest inspiration.

To my amazing children, Moroni, Nephi, Racheal, and Daniel, who continue to fill my life with joy, purpose, and pride. You are each a shining example of resilience, curiosity, and kindness. Watching you grow and pursue your dreams has been one of my greatest joys, and I dedicate this book to the bright futures you all have ahead of you.

To my wonderful daughters-in-law, Tausala and Jessica, you have brought so much love and happiness into our family. Your warmth and spirit have enriched our lives and strengthened our family bond. I am so grateful to have you both as part of this journey.

And to my dear grandson, William, and all the future grandchildren who will one day join our family, this book is for you, too. May you always feel empowered to make wise decisions and live a life full of love, laughter, and fulfillment. I look forward to the day you will join our family and bring your unique light into our lives.

- David Okonah

ISBN: 978-1-965551-00-4

Contents

Introduction

How to Make Insurance Work for You: A Personal Finance Guide is here to change how you think about insurance. If the word "insurance" makes you want to yawn and reach for the nearest cup of green tea, you are not alone. But stick with me—this book is designed to make insurance understandable and relevant to your life. Think of it as your roadmap to financial peace of mind-clear, practical, and enjoyable to read.

This book aims to demystify the insurance world and show you how to use it as a powerful tool in your personal finance arsenal. We will cover everything from understanding the basics to choosing the right insurance, avoiding pitfalls, navigating claims, and staying ahead of industry trends using everyday examples. By the end, you will be equipped to make informed decisions that protect your finances and support your personal growth.

How Insurance Fits into Personal Finance

Insurance might not be the most glamorous aspect of personal finance, but it is essential. Think of it as the safety net in your financial circus act. Without it, one misstep—a car accident, a health emergency, or a house fire—could put you into financial ruin. With the right insurance, you can confidently walk the high wire of life, knowing that you have a net to catch you if you stumble.

Imagine you are Sarah, a 32-year-old nurse and a self-improvement enthusiast. You have been diligently saving for a down payment on your dream home. Suddenly, you get into a car accident, and the repair costs threaten to drain your savings. Fortunately, your auto insurance covers most expenses and keeps your home-buying plans on track.

Importance of Making Informed Insurance Decisions

Making informed insurance decisions is crucial. The wrong choice can leave you unprotected and overpaying, while the right choice can save you money and provide peace of mind. This book will guide you through assessing your needs, choosing the right policies, and maximizing your benefits—all tailored to your lifestyle. What You'll Learn.

Here is a sneak peek at what is inside:

Chapter One: We'll start by breaking down the basics, helping you understand what insurance is and why it's crucial.

Chapter Two: Learn how to assess your insurance needs based on your unique life situation.

Chapter Three: Dive into life insurance and discover how to choose the best policy for your needs.

Chapter Four: Navigate the complexities of health insurance with practical tips and examples.

Chapter Five: Get to grips with auto and home insurance essentials, ensuring you're fully protected.

Chapter Six: Understand the importance of disability and long-term care insurance for your future security.

Chapter Seven: Take a moment to share your thoughts and review what you've learned so far.

Chapter Eight: Protect yourself and your property with a comprehensive look at renters and landlord insurance.

Chapter Nine: Discover how annuities can secure your financial future as you age.

Chapter Ten: Simplify Medicare Insurance Plans to make the best choices for your healthcare needs.

Chapter Eleven: Learn how to maximize your insurance benefits while minimizing costs.

Chapter Twelve: Master the ins and outs of filing claims and avoiding common pitfalls.

Chapter Thirteen: Discover the importance of regularly reviewing and updating your insurance policies.

Chapter Fourteen: Explore the future of insurance and personal finance, from AI to blockchain.

Chapter Fifteen: Write a final review and reflect on everything you've learned.

By the end of this book, you will understand how to make insurance work for you and feel empowered to take control of your financial future. Please sit back, relax, and let us simplify the insurance world.

Chapter One

Understanding the Basics of Insurance

"Risk comes from not knowing what you're doing"
– Warren Buffett

Insurance is a crucial part of any well-rounded personal finance strategy. Yet, for many people, the insurance world seems daunting and complex. This chapter will explain insurance, providing you with a solid foundation of knowledge that will help you make informed decisions and integrate insurance seamlessly into your financial plans.

What is Insurance?

At its core, insurance is a way to manage risk. Life is full of uncertainties—accidents, illnesses, natural disasters, etc. Insurance provides financial protection against these unforeseen events. You transfer the risk of a significant economic loss to the insurance company by paying a premium. In return, the insurer agrees to compensate you if a covered event occurs.

Think of insurance as a safety net. Imagine you are walking on a tightrope. Without a safety net, a fall could be disastrous. But with a safety net in place, even if you stumble, you know there is something to catch you and prevent serious harm. Insurance acts as that safety net for various aspects of your life.

Types of Insurance

There are various types of insurance, each designed to protect different areas of your life. Here are some of the most common types:

1. Life Insurance
2. Health Insurance
3. Auto Insurance
4. Home Insurance
5. Renters and Landlord's Insurance
5. Disability Insurance
6. Long-Term Care Insurance
7. Medicare Insurance

Let us delve into each type briefly.

Life Insurance

Life insurance provides financial protection for your loved ones in the event of your death. The primary goal is to replace lost income and cover expenses like education, housing, funerals, debts, and living costs for your dependents.

Health Insurance

Health insurance pays for medical expenses like doctor visits, hospital stays, surgeries, and prescriptions. It is vital because medical costs can be incredibly high, and having coverage can save you from financial ruin.

Auto Insurance

Auto insurance protects you against economic loss in case of a vehicle accident. It can cover damage to your car, medical expenses, and liability costs if you injure someone or damage their property.

Home Insurance

Home insurance protects your home and belongings against fire, theft, and natural disasters. Also, it provides liability protection if someone gets injured on your property.

Renter's and Landlord's Insurance

Renters insurance protects tenants by covering their personal belongings and providing liability coverage in case of damage or injury within their rental property. It typically includes protection against theft, fire, and certain water damage, ensuring unexpected incidents do not financially burden renters.

Landlord insurance, on the other hand, is tailored for property owners who rent out their spaces. It covers the physical structure of the rental property, offers liability protection if a tenant or visitor is injured on the property, and often includes loss of rental income if the property becomes uninhabitable due to covered events. These insurances provide essential protection for both renters and landlords, securing personal property, maintaining financial stability, and safeguarding against potential legal and repair costs.

Disability Insurance

Disability insurance replaces a portion of your income if you cannot work because of illness or injury. This type of insurance ensures you can maintain your standard of living even when you cannot earn an income.

Long-Term Care Insurance

Long-term care insurance pays for the cost of care when you have a chronic illness or disability that requires long-term help. This insurance can pay for care at home, nursing homes, or assisted living facilities.

Medicare Insurance

Medicare is a federal health insurance program primarily for people aged 65 and older, as well as certain younger individuals with disabilities. It includes Part A (hospital insurance) and Part B (medical insurance) for essential healthcare services like hospital stays, doctor visits, and preventive care. Additionally, Medicare Part C, also known as Medicare Advantage, is an alternative that combines Parts A and B, often with additional benefits like prescription drug coverage and vision, dental, and hearing care. Medicare also offers Part D for stand-alone prescription drug coverage through private insurance and Medigap plans to help with out-of-pocket costs, ensuring comprehensive healthcare coverage that supports seniors and those with disabilities in managing their health needs effectively.

Key Insurance Concepts

To fully understand insurance, it is essential to grasp a few key concepts. Let us break down some of the most important terms you will encounter.

Premium

A premium is the amount you pay to an insurance company for your insurance policy. You can pay premiums monthly, quarterly, or annually, depending on the terms of your policy.

Think of your premium as a subscription fee. Just like you pay a monthly fee for a streaming service to watch movies and TV shows, you pay a premium to keep your insurance coverage active.

Deductible

A deductible is the amount you must pay out of pocket for covered services before your insurance coverage starts. Higher deductibles typically lead to lower premiums and vice versa.

Imagine you have auto insurance with a $1000 deductible. If you are in an accident and the repair costs are $3,000, you would pay the first $1000, and your insurance company would cover the remaining $2000.

Coverage

Coverage refers to the specific protection your insurance policy provides. This protection can include the losses covered, the amount of money the insurer will pay, and any exclusions.

If you have health insurance, it may cover doctor visits, hospital stays, and prescription medications. However, it might exclude specific experimental treatments or cosmetic procedures.

Policy Limit

The policy limit is the maximum amount any insurance company will pay for a covered loss when the unexpected happens. There can be limits per claim, incident, or over the policy's life.

For example, if your home insurance policy has a limit of $300,000 and a fire causes $350,000 damage, you are responsible for $50,000.

Beneficiary

A beneficiary is a person or entity designated to receive the insurance payout. This term is mostly used in life insurance policies.

For instance, you might name your spouse as the beneficiary if you have a life insurance policy. Your spouse will receive the payout for the policy in the event of your death.

The Importance of Insurance in Personal Finance

Insurance plays a vital role in a comprehensive personal finance plan. Here is why:

1. Protection Against Major Financial Losses

Insurance can prevent you from suffering devastating financial losses. Whether it is a car accident, a major illness, or damage to your home, having insurance ensures you will not have to bear the entire financial burden alone.

2. Peace of Mind

Knowing you have insurance coverage can provide peace of mind. It allows you to live without worrying about what might happen if disaster strikes.

3. Financial Planning and Security

Insurance helps with long-term financial planning. Providing a safety net that protects your assets and income ensures that unforeseen events do not derail your financial goals.

4. Meeting Legal and Contractual Obligations

Some types of insurance, like auto and home insurance, are required by law or lenders. Having the necessary coverage ensures you comply with these requirements.

Consider John, who has a young family and a mortgage. He takes out life insurance and homeowners insurance policies to ensure that if anything happens to him, his family can continue to live comfortably and pay off the mortgage with the payout from the life insurance while the homeowners' proceeds help to rebuild their home. This policy gives John peace of mind, knowing his loved ones are protected financially.

Common Myths and Misconceptions about Insurance

Despite its importance, there are many myths and misconceptions about insurance. Let us address a few of these to help clear up any confusion.

Myth 1: I am Young and Healthy, So I Do Not Need Insurance

Young, healthy individuals may face lower risks, but illnesses, disasters, and accidents can happen to anyone at any time. Having insurance ensures you are prepared for the unexpected event.

Myth 2: Insurance is Too Expensive

The cost of insurance can vary widely depending on the type, your age, and where you live, but many affordable options are available. Shopping around and comparing policies is essential to finding one that fits your budget. The financial protection insurance provides can far outweigh the cost of premiums.

Myth 3: I Don't Need Life Insurance Because I am Single

Even if you are single, life insurance can still be valuable. It can cover funeral expenses, pay off debts, and provide financial support to any dependents you may have, such as aging parents or siblings.

Myth 4: Insurance Companies Always Try to Avoid Paying Claims

While insurance companies must manage their risk, they must also adhere to the regulations and laws of the state and act in good faith. To ensure you receive the coverage you are entitled to, you must familiarize yourself with your policy and partner with reputable insurance companies.

How to Get Started with Insurance

Getting started with insurance does not have to be overwhelming. Here are some simple steps to help you on your journey:

1. Assess Your Needs

Consider your personal and financial situation. What risks do you face? What assets do you need to protect?

2. Research and Compare Policies

Look into the different types of insurance and the policies available. Compare coverage options, premiums, and insurers to find the best fit for your needs.

3. Seek Professional Advice

If you are still determining what type of insurance you need or how much coverage you should get, consider speaking with a financial advisor or insurance agent. They can provide personalized recommendations based on your situation.

4. Read the Fine Print

Carefully read the terms and conditions of any policy you are considering. Ensure you understand what is covered, excluded, and any limitations or conditions.

5. Start with the Basics

If you are new to insurance, start with the essential types: health, auto, home, and life insurance. As you become more comfortable, you can explore additional coverage options.

Insurance is an essential tool for managing risk and protecting your financial future. Understanding insurance basics will allow you to make informed decisions and integrate them into your personal finance strategy. Insurance offers a safety net enabling you to live your life confidently, knowing you are protected.

In the following chapters, we will delve deeper into each type of insurance, providing you with the knowledge and tools you need to make insurance work for you. This guide is here to assist you in understanding insurance, whether you are a beginner or looking to review your current policy.

Chapter Two

Assessing Your Insurance Needs

"The best investment you can make is an investment in yourself."

– Warren Buffett

In our bustling world, assessing your insurance needs can feel like just another item on your ever-growing to-do list. It is essential to take the time to understand the insurance you need and how much coverage is necessary to protect your finances. This chapter provides a simple approach to evaluating your insurance needs, using examples that relate to your everyday life.

Why Assessing Your Insurance Needs is Important

Insurance is not a one-size-fits-all solution. Your needs will vary based on your life stage, family situation, career, and personal goals. To ensure you are spending less on insurance, carefully evaluate your needs and get the right coverage for you and your family.

Think of insurance like clothing. Just as you would not wear a winter coat in the summer, you do not need the same insurance coverage at all stages of your life. Assessing your needs helps you "dress" appropriately for your financial situation.

Life Stages and Insurance Needs

Different life stages bring different priorities and risks. Here is a breakdown of how your insurance needs might evolve:

Early Career (Ages 25-35)

Health Insurance: Essential for covering medical expenses.

Auto Insurance: This is a must-have by law if you own a car.

Renters Insurance: Protect your belongings if you rent your home.

Disability Insurance: Provides income when you cannot work because of illness or injury.

Starting a Family (Ages 30-40)

Life Insurance: Critical to protect your family's financial future.

Health Insurance: Continued importance, especially with children.

Homeowners Insurance: If you buy a home, this covers damages and liability.

Disability Insurance: Ensures financial stability if you cannot work.

Established Career and Family (Ages 35-45)

Life Insurance: You may need to increase coverage as your financial responsibilities grow.

Health Insurance: Ongoing necessity.

Homeowners Insurance: Maintain and update as needed.

Long-Term Care Insurance: Start considering future health needs.

Family and Retirement (Ages 64-70)

Life Insurance: Evaluate your life Insurance needs; you may consider final expense insurance for funeral expenses.

Medicare Insurance: Consider Medicare, Medicare plans, or Medigap, and Part D

Homeowners Insurance: Maintain and update as needed

Long-Term Care Insurance: Maintain and update as needed.

Determining the Right Amount of Coverage

Once you have identified the types of insurance you need, the next step is determining the appropriate amount of coverage. Here are some guidelines to help you:

Life Insurance

To calculate how much life insurance you need, consider the following factors:

Income Replacement: Multiply your annual income by the number of years you want to provide for your family.

Debt Repayment: Include mortgages, car loans, and other debts.

Education Costs: Estimate future education expenses for your children.

Living Expenses: Consider day-to-day expenses your family will need to cover.

Take, for instance, Jane, a 35-year-old mother of two with an annual income of $60,000. She wants to ensure her family is covered for ten years. She also has a $200,000 mortgage and expects to spend $100,000 on her children's education. Jane's life insurance coverage calculation:

Income Replacement: $60,000 x 10 = $600,000

Debt Repayment: $200,000

Education Costs: $100,000

Total Coverage Needed: $900,000

Health Insurance

When selecting health insurance, consider the following factors:

Monthly Premiums: Ensure they fit within your budget.

Deductibles and Out-of-Pocket Costs: Higher deductibles often mean lower premiums but more expenses if you need care.

Coverage Needs: To avoid surprises, check if your preferred doctors are in the network and if your medications are covered as generic or brand names.

Tom, who is 30 years old, is a professional in his field. He chooses a health plan with a $200 monthly premium, a $1,000 deductible, and an 80/20 coinsurance. He expects to visit the doctor a few times a year and wants his medication covered. This balance of costs and coverage suits his needs.

Homeowners or Renters Insurance

Consider the value of your home and belongings, plus any potential liability issues:

Replacement cost: This covers all the expenses associated with repairing or replacing your home and belongings, while actual cash value factors in depreciation.

Liability Coverage: Ensures protection if someone sustains an injury on your property.

Erika, a 32-year-old homeowner, owns a home valued at $300,000 and belongings worth $50,000. To ensure complete protection, she opts for replacement cost coverage and includes $300,000 in liability coverage.

Special Considerations for Busy Professionals

As a busy professional, time is a precious commodity. Here are some tips to streamline the process of assessing and securing your insurance needs:

Use Online Tools and Resources

Many insurance companies offer online calculators and resources to help you estimate your coverage needs. Take advantage of these tools to save time and simplify the process.

Work with an Insurance Agent

An insurance agent can provide personalized advice and help you navigate the various options. They can save you time by doing the legwork and finding the best policies for your situation. Choose your agent wisely.

Regularly Review Your Policies

Life changes quickly, and your insurance needs may evolve. Schedule an annual review of your policies to ensure they meet your needs. This annual review is critical after significant life events such as marriage, having children, buying a home, or changing jobs.

For example, a 28-year-old project manager, Emily, uses an online life insurance calculator to estimate her coverage needs. She then consults with an insurance agent to find the best policy. She reviews her insurance with her agent yearly to ensure it aligns with her changing life circumstances.

Common Insurance Pitfalls to Avoid

Even with careful planning, there are common pitfalls to watch out for when assessing your insurance needs. Here are some tips to help you avoid them:

Underinsuring

One of the biggest mistakes is needing more insurance coverage. Under-insuring can leave you vulnerable to significant financial losses. Always err on caution and get slightly more coverage than you need.

Over Insuring

Conversely, over-insuring can lead to unnecessary expenses. While adequate coverage is essential, paying for excessive insurance can strain your budget. Find a balance that provides sufficient protection without overextending your finances. Your insurance broker can help you during your annual review.

Mike, a 40-year-old teacher, initially underinsured his home with only $200,000 in coverage. After reassessing with his agent, he realized the replacement cost was $300,000. Mike adjusted his policy to ensure complete protection. He followed his agent's advice to avoid over-insurance and opted for a $1 million life insurance policy instead of $2 million.

Ignoring Policy Details

It is crucial to read and understand the details of your insurance policies. Pay attention to coverage limits, exclusions, and conditions. Understanding what is and needs to be covered can prevent unpleasant surprises when making a claim.

Not Updating Policies

As mentioned earlier, regularly reviewing and updating your policies is essential. Failing to do so can result in outdated coverage that no longer meets your needs.

Anna, a 37-year-old marketing executive, failed to update her life insurance policy after having twins. She realized that her coverage needed to be improved for her expanded family. After reviewing her needs, she increased her coverage to secure her children's future and updated the beneficiary information to include the twins.

Using Insurance to Achieve Financial Goals

Insurance is more than just protection; it is a tool to reach financial goals. Here is how:

Building Wealth with Life Insurance

Some life insurance policies, like Whole Life, Index Whole Life, or Universal Life, have a cash value component that can grow. This policy can help you build wealth while ensuring financial protection for your family.

David, a 35-year-old engineer, purchases an Index whole life insurance policy. In addition to providing a death benefit, the policy accumulates cash value over time as the index performs well to reach the cap or remain on the guaranteed minimum interest rate in a bad year. David can borrow against this cash value for future expenses, such as his children's education, or as a retirement income.

Planning for Healthcare Costs

Health insurance can be a critical part of your financial planning, especially as healthcare costs continue to rise. Choosing the right health plan and using health savings accounts (HSAs) can help you manage these expenses more effectively.

For example, a 29-year-old graphic designer named Maria chooses a high-deductible health plan paired with an HSA. She contributes to the HSA regularly, building a tax-advantaged fund to cover future medical expenses.

Protecting Your Home and Investments

Homeowner's insurance protects your home and can safeguard your financial investment. Ensuring adequate coverage can prevent significant financial setbacks if your home is damaged or destroyed.

Let us consider Carlos, a 42-year-old IT manager who invests in rental properties. He ensures each property has comprehensive homeowners' insurance to protect his investments from potential risks like fire, theft, or natural disasters.

Assessing your insurance needs is a crucial step in securing your financial future. Understanding the various insurance options and selecting the right coverage can shield you and your loved ones from unexpected financial hardships. Insurance is an essential part of your financial strategy. Review it regularly to keep it up to date with your changing circumstances.

In the next chapter, we will explore the process of selecting the best insurance policies, providing you with the tools and knowledge to make informed decisions. Whether you are a busy professional, a parent, or someone looking to improve your financial security, this guide will help you navigate the insurance world with confidence and ease.

Chapter Three

Choosing the Right Life Insurance Policy

"Price is what you pay. Value is what you get."

– Warren Buffett

L ife insurance is one of the most critical financial tools for personal finance. However, choosing the right life insurance policy can be overwhelming due to the various options available. This chapter will guide you through selecting the best life insurance policy for your needs, using simple and relatable examples to make complex concepts easy to understand. Business professionals, parents, and anyone looking to buy insurance would benefit significantly from studying this book.

Why Life Insurance is Important

Life insurance provides financial security for your loved ones in the event of your sudden death. It ensures that they can maintain their standard of living, pay off debts, and cover future expenses such as education and healthcare. Life insurance can also be a tool for building wealth and achieving long-term financial goals.

Imagine you are a 35-year-old parent with two young children. You want to ensure that if anything happens to you, your family can continue living in your home, your kids can go to college, and your spouse will not be burdened with financial stress. Life insurance provides the financial cushion to make this possible.

Types of Life Insurance

There are two primary types of life insurance: term life insurance and permanent life insurance. Each type has its features, benefits, and drawbacks.

Term Life Insurance

Term life insurance covers a specific period, usually 10, 20, or 30 years. Should you pass away during the term, the insurance company will pay out the death benefit to your beneficiaries. If you outlive the term, the policy expires, and the insurance company pays no benefits.

Pros:

- Affordable premiums

- Straightforward coverage

- Ideal for temporary needs (e.g., paying off a mortgage)

Cons:

- No cash value accumulation

- Coverage ends when the term expires.

- Change in a health condition could negatively impact future coverage.

For example, Sarah, a 30-year-old teacher, buys a 20-year term life insurance policy with a $1000,000 death benefit. She pays $35 per month in premiums. If Sarah dies within the 20-year term, her beneficiaries will receive $1000,000. If she outlives the term, the policy ends, and she gets no benefits. If Sarah is diagnosed with cancer after 20 years, it may be difficult, if not impossible, to buy another life insurance policy with the same face amount.

Permanent Life Insurance

Permanent life insurance covers your entire life if you pay the premiums. There are several types of permanent life insurance, including whole life, Index whole life, universal life, and variable life insurance. These policies often include a cash value component that grows over time.

Pros:

- Lifetime coverage

- Cash value accumulation.

- It can be used as an investment tool.

Cons:

- Higher premiums compared to term life insurance.

- More complex policies

- Potential for lower returns compared to other investments.

- Policy loans and withdrawals come with interest and fees.

Let us consider Barry, a 40-year-old civil engineer who buys a whole life insurance policy with a $200,000 death benefit. He pays $150 per month in premiums. Over time, Barry's policy accumulates cash value, which he can borrow against or use for other financial needs. If he dies at any age, his beneficiaries receive the $200,000 death benefit minus the interest payments.

Factors to Consider When Choosing a Life Insurance Policy

When choosing a life insurance policy, consider the following factors to ensure you select the best option for your needs:

Your Financial Goals

Determine what you want your life insurance policy to achieve. Are you looking to provide financial security for your family, pay off debts, save for college, pay off your mortgage, or build wealth? Your goals will influence the type of policy you choose. Whether you choose term, permanent, variable, or index life insurance, conducting a need-based analysis would save you a lot of money and frustration in the future. Before meeting with your insurance advisor to explore your options, ensure you know what you want in a life insurance policy. Avoid a pushy insurance advisor who does not seek to understand you first.

Coverage Amount

Calculate the coverage you need based on your financial responsibilities and future goals. Remember to think about your healthcare, long-term care, income replacement, debt repayment, and future expenses.

Premiums

Evaluate your budget to determine how much you can pay in premiums. While term life insurance premiums are lower, permanent life insurance offers additional benefits.

Policy Features

Consider the features and benefits of each policy type. For example, permanent life insurance may be better if you want a policy that accumulates cash value.

For instance, a 32-year-old marketing manager named Maria wants to ensure her family's financial security if she passes away. She calculates that her family would need $700,000 to cover her children's income replacement, mortgage, and future education expenses. She decides to purchase a 20-year term life insurance policy with a $700,000 death benefit, paying $30 monthly in premiums. This policy aligns with her financial goals and budget.

Comparing Term and Permanent Life Insurance

To help you make an informed decision, let us compare terms and permanent life insurance in more detail.

Term Life Insurance

- This policy is intended for individuals needing temporary financial assistance, seeking affordable coverage, or preferring straightforward policies.

- It has a fixed duration (e.g., 10, 20, 30 years).

- This option offers lower premiums, which can help you save on costs. This policy focuses purely on the death benefit provided by the coverage.

For example, a 28-year-old Flight attendant named Mark buys a 20-year term life insurance policy with a $1 million death benefit. He pays $40 per month in premiums. This policy will protect his family if Mark dies during his peak earning years.

Permanent Life Insurance

This coverage is ideal for those who want lifelong protection, policies with cash value, and investment options. It provides lifelong protection, but the cost of this service is associated with higher premiums. The coverage provides both death benefits plus cash value accumulation.

For example, a 45-year-old business owner named Lisa buys a universal life insurance policy with a $250,000 death benefit. She pays $200 per month in premiums. Over time, her policy accumulates cash value, which she can use for business investments or personal expenses. Her beneficiaries receive the death benefit when she passes away.

Tips for Choosing the Right Life Insurance Policy

To help you choose the best life insurance policy that would suit your needs, here are some practical tips:

1. Assess Your Financial Situation

Look closely at your financial situation, including your income, debts, and future expenses. This assessment will help you determine the coverage you need and the type of policy that fits your budget.

2. Consider Your Life Stage

Your insurance needs will change as you move through different life stages. For example, a young professional may need less coverage than someone with a family and a mortgage. Consider your current life stage and future goals when choosing a policy.

For everyday example, John, a 27-year-old graphic designer, is single with no children. He purchases a 20-year term life insurance policy with a $250,000 death benefit to cover his student loans and provide a financial cushion for his parents. As his life circumstances change, he can adjust his coverage as needed.

3. Compare Multiple Policies

Refrain from settling for the first policy you come across. Compare multiple policies from different insurers to find the best coverage and premiums. Use online comparison tools or work with an insurance agent to explore your options.

4. Understand Policy Terms and Conditions

Read the terms and conditions of any policy you are considering. Ensure you understand the coverage, exclusions, and potential fees or penalties. Understanding your policy will help you avoid surprises and choose a policy that meets your needs.

For example, Emma, a 35-year-old nurse, compares three different insurers' term and permanent life insurance policies. She carefully reviews each policy's terms and conditions, paying attention to coverage limits, exclusions, and premium costs. This thorough comparison helps her choose a policy that gives her family the best value and protection.

5. Seek Professional Advice

If you need help to decide which policy to buy, seek advice from a financial advisor or insurance agent. They can provide personalized recommendations based on your financial situation and goals.

Let us consider Robert, a 40-year-old accountant who consults with a financial advisor to determine the best life insurance policy for his needs. The advisor helps him understand the benefits of term and permanent life insurance and recommends a policy that aligns with his long-term financial goals. Rob can contact his local licensed agent or reach out to the insurance office.

Common Misconceptions About Life Insurance

Several misconceptions about life insurance can lead to confusion and poor decision-making. Let us debunk some of these myths:

Myth 1: Life Insurance is Only for older adults

There's a belief that life insurance is only essential for older people. Life insurance is vital for anyone with financial dependents or significant debts. The earlier you purchase life insurance, the lower your premiums will be.

For example, Jennifer, a 29-year-old lawyer, buys a term life insurance policy with a $400,000 death benefit. Her premiums are low because she is young and healthy. If she had waited until she was older, her premiums would be higher, and she might have health conditions that could affect her coverage.

Myth 2: Employer-Provided Life Insurance is Sufficient

While employer-provided life insurance is valuable, it may need to provide more coverage to meet your needs. You may lose your coverage if you change jobs. It is essential to have a personal life insurance policy to ensure continuous protection.

For instance, a 33-year-old sales manager, Tom has a life insurance policy through his employer that provides a $100,000 death benefit. However, he realizes this cannot cover his mortgage and his children's future education expenses. Tom purchases an additional $500,000 term life insurance policy to ensure his family is fully protected.

Myth 3: Stay-at-Home Parents Don't Need Life Insurance

Stay-at-home parents offer priceless support to their families; if they are not there, it would be financially and emotionally costly. Life insurance can help cover childcare, household expenses, and other costs if a stay-at-home parent dies.

Let us consider Linda, a 37-year-old stay-at-home mom, who purchased a $300,000 term life insurance policy. This coverage allows her husband to cover childcare and household responsibilities if something happens to her so he can keep working and supporting their family.

Myth 4: Life Insurance is Too Expensive

Many people overestimate the cost of life insurance and assume it is unaffordable. However, term life insurance policies are often affordable, especially for young and healthy individuals. It is worth exploring your options to find a policy that fits your budget.

James, a 28-year-old web developer, assumes life insurance will be too expensive. After researching, he finds a 20-year term life insurance policy with a $500,000 death benefit for just $20 per month. This affordable policy provides essential financial protection for his family.

The Application Process

Applying for life insurance includes filling out an application, having a medical exam, and waiting for approval. Here is the summary of the application process:

1. Complete the Application

Provide accurate information about your personal and medical history, lifestyle, and financial situation. This information helps insurance companies assess your risk and determine your premiums.

2. Undergo a Medical Exam

Most life insurance applications require a medical exam to evaluate your health. The exam comprises the measurements of your weight, height, blood pressure, and blood tests. Simplified issue or guaranteed issue life insurance policies skip the medical exam, but you will have to pay more for less coverage.

3. Review and Approval

The insurance company reviews your application and medical exam results to determine your eligibility and premiums. This process can take several weeks. Once your insurance application is approved, they will send you the policy document, and you can start making premium payments to keep your coverage active.

For example, Samantha, a 34-year-old teacher, applies for a term life insurance policy. She completes the application, providing details about her medical history and lifestyle. She schedules a medical exam, which includes measurements and blood tests. After a few weeks, she receives approval and her policy documents, confirming her coverage.

Policy Riders and Additional Benefits

Life insurance policies often offer optional riders that provide additional benefits and customization. Here are some standard riders to consider:

Accelerated Death Benefit Rider

This rider permits the insured to access a portion of the death benefit when diagnosed with a terminal illness. This rider benefit can help cover medical expenses and provide financial support during a challenging time.

Waiver of Premium Rider

If you become disabled and unable to work, this rider waives your life insurance premiums, ensuring your coverage remains active without additional financial strain.

Guaranteed Insurability Rider

This rider allows you to purchase additional coverage at specified intervals without undergoing a medical exam. It is helpful if you anticipate needing more coverage in the future.

Accidental Death Benefit Rider

This rider provides an additional death benefit if you die because of an accident. It is an affordable way to increase your coverage for accidental deaths.

For example, Michael, a 38-year-old high school janitor, adds a waiver of premium rider to his term life insurance policy. If he becomes disabled and unable to work, he will not have to worry about paying his life insurance premiums, ensuring his family's financial protection.

Reviewing and Updating Your Policy

Life is full of changes, and your insurance needs may evolve. Regular review and updates of your life insurance policy are essential to ensure it continues to meet your needs.

1. Schedule Regular Reviews

Remember to review your life insurance policy annually or after significant life events like marriage, childbirth, or a home purchase.

2. Adjust Coverage as Needed

If your financial responsibilities or goals change, adjust your coverage accordingly. This policy review may involve increasing or decreasing your death benefit, changing your policy type, or adding riders.

3. Keep Beneficiary Information Up to Date

Ensure your beneficiary information is current. Beneficiary updates include adding new beneficiaries, such as a spouse or child, and removing no longer relevant individuals.

Let us consider Rachel, a 31-year-old nurse who reviews her term life insurance policy annually. After the birth of her second child, she decides to increase her coverage to ensure both children are financially protected. She updates her policy and beneficiary information to reflect on her growing family.

Selecting the right life insurance policy ensures your financial future and protects your loved ones. To make an intelligent decision about life insurance, study the policy types, consider your needs, and compare policies. Remember to review and update your policy regularly to ensure it continues to meet your evolving needs. With the right life insurance policy, you can enjoy peace of mind knowing that your family is financially protected, no matter what the future holds.

In the next chapter, we will delve into the process of selecting health insurance, providing you with the knowledge and tools to navigate this essential aspect of your financial planning. Regardless of your stage in life, this guide will help you make confident and informed decisions about your health insurance coverage.

Chapter Four

Navigating Health Insurance

"An investment in knowledge pays the best interest."
– Benjamin Franklin

Health insurance is an essential component of personal finance and overall well-being. It protects against high medical costs, ensuring you can access the care you need without financial hardship. However, navigating health insurance can be complex and overwhelming, especially with various plans and options available. This chapter will guide you through the basics of health insurance, helping you understand key concepts and choose the right plan for your needs. Using simple, everyday examples, we aim to make this topic accessible and enjoyable for you.

Why Health Insurance Matters

Health insurance is vital in safeguarding your physical well-being and financial security. It is a safety net, ensuring you can access medical care without shouldering exorbitant costs. From covering routine doctor visits and hospital stays to providing financial assistance for prescriptions and preventive care, health insurance offers comprehensive support for various healthcare needs.

For example, imagine you are a 30-year-old waitress named Emma. One day, you wake up with severe abdominal pain and need to visit the emergency room. Without health insurance, the cost of the ER visit, diagnostic tests, and treatment could be thousands of dollars. Health insurance covers some of these costs, reducing out-of-pocket expenses and financial stress.

Understanding Health Insurance Terms

Before choosing a health insurance plan, one must understand some key terms commonly used in the industry. These terms will help you make informed decisions and better navigate your options.

Premium

The amount you pay for your health insurance policy to an insurance organization is typically monthly, but it could also be quarterly or annually. Ask about discounts if you decide to pay annually.

Deductible

The amount you must pay out-of-pocket first to your health providers before the covered medical services your insurance plan pays.

Co-payment (Copay)

The co-payment is a predetermined fee that you pay to your health providers for covered healthcare services when you receive them.

Coinsurance

The percentage of costs you pay for covered services after you have met your deductible. For example, if your coinsurance is 20%, you pay 20% of the cost of the service to your healthcare providers, and your insurance pays the remaining 80%.

Out-of-Pocket Maximum

This is the maximum amount you need to pay your healthcare providers for covered services in a year. Once you reach this limit, your insurance covers 100% of the costs for covered services.

Network

A group of doctors, hospitals, and other healthcare providers agreed to provide services at discounted rates for members of a health insurance plan.

For example, John, a 35-year-old teacher, has a health insurance plan with a $500 monthly premium, a $1,000 deductible, a $20 copay for doctor visits, and 20% coinsurance. His out-of-pocket maximum is $5,000. Understanding these terms helps John anticipate his healthcare costs and manage his budget effectively.

Types of Health Insurance Plans

There are several health insurance plans, each with features, benefits, and limitations. The most common types are Health Maintenance Organizations (HMOs), Preferred Provider Organizations (PPOs), Exclusive Provider Organizations (EPOs), and High-Deductible Health Plans (HDHPs), often paired with Health Savings Accounts (HSAs).

Health Maintenance Organization (HMO)

- **Features:** You must choose a primary care physician (PCP) who coordinates your care and provides referrals to specialists. Typically, it would help if you used providers within the HMO network.

- This plan's advantages include reduced premiums, out-of-pocket costs, and a strong focus on preventive care.

- The drawbacks are the limited provider network and the need for a referral to see specialists.

Joan, a 28-year-old nurse, chooses an HMO plan because it offers lower premiums and values the emphasis on preventive care. She selects a primary care physician who coordinates her care and provides referrals when needed.

Preferred Provider Organization (PPO)

- **Features**: Offers more flexibility in choosing providers and specialists. You can see any doctor or specialist without a referral, both in and out of the network, though you will pay less for in-network providers.

- Pros: Greater flexibility in choosing providers, no need for referrals.

- Cons: Higher premiums and out-of-pocket costs compared to HMOs.

Jonathan, a 40-year-old pilot, prefers a PPO plan because it allows him to see any specialist without a referral. He appreciates the flexibility, even though it comes with higher premiums.

Exclusive Provider Organization (EPO)

- **Features**: Similar to a PPO but without coverage for out-of-network providers, except in emergencies.

- Pros: Lower premiums than PPOs, so there is no need for referrals.

- Cons: No out-of-network coverage.

Vivian, a 32-year-old freelance actress, opts for an EPO plan because it balances cost and flexibility. She is willing to stay within the network to keep her premiums lower.

High-Deductible Health Plan (HDHP) with Health Savings Account (HSA)

- **Features**: HDHPs have higher deductibles and lower premiums. The HDHP can be paired with an HSA, a tax-advantaged savings account for medical expenses.

- HDHP offers lower premiums, tax advantages with an HSA, and the potential for long-term savings. Contact your local bank to find out how to open an HSA account after enrollment in HDHP.

- The drawback of the plan is the higher out-of-pocket costs to meet the deductible.

David, a 38-year-old entrepreneur, chooses an HDHP paired with an HSA. He appreciates the lower premiums and the ability to save pre-tax dollars for future medical expenses. He uses his HSA to pay for routine medical costs and save for unexpected health issues like dental care, prescriptions, etc.

Assessing Your Health Insurance Needs

Assessing your needs and priorities is essential when choosing a health insurance plan. Consider your health status, budget, preferred doctors and hospitals, and the services you use most frequently.

Health Status

Evaluate your current health status and any ongoing medical conditions. If you have chronic health issues or need regular medical care, a plan with lower out-of-pocket costs and comprehensive coverage might be best.

For example, Laura, a 33-year-old accountant with asthma, requires regular check-ups and medication. She chooses a PPO plan that offers broader coverage to see providers in the network and lower out-of-pocket costs for her ongoing care. She can also visit providers outside the network with a higher copay. That flexibility appeals to her needs.

Budget

Determine how much you can spend on premiums, deductibles, co-pay, and coinsurance. Balancing monthly premiums with potential out-of-pocket costs is crucial for managing your overall healthcare expenses.

Michael, a 29-year-old freelance writer, is relatively healthy, takes no medications, and has a limited budget. He selects an HDHP with lower premiums and uses his HSA to cover routine medical expenses, minimizing overall costs on the total annual premium.

Preferred Providers

Ensure your preferred doctors or hospitals are included in the plan's network. Some plans, like HMOs and EPOs, have more restrictive networks, while PPOs offer greater flexibility.

For example, Anna, a 36-year-old lawyer, prefers to continue seeing her long-time primary care physician and specialist. She chooses a PPO plan that includes her preferred providers in the network, ensuring she can maintain her current care with her doctor.

Types of Services

Consider the most frequently used services, such as preventive care, specialist visits, or prescription medications. Choose a plan that provides good coverage for these services.

Brian, a 41-year-old architect, frequently needs physical therapy for a previous injury. He selects a plan with comprehensive coverage for specialist visits and physical therapy, ensuring his ongoing care is affordable and covered.

Comparing Health Insurance Plans

To find the best health insurance plan for your needs, compare multiple plans based on critical factors such as premiums, deductibles, copays, coinsurance, out-of-pocket maximums, and provider networks.

Premiums

Compare the monthly premiums for different plans. Lower premiums can be attractive, but consider the plan's overall cost, including deductibles and out-of-pocket expenses.

Natalie, a 30-year-old teacher, compares two plans: one with a $300 monthly premium and a $1,500 deductible and another with a $200 monthly premium and a $3,000 deductible. She calculates her potential out-of-pocket costs for both plans to determine which offers the best value for her needs.

Deductibles

Evaluate the deductibles for each plan. Higher deductibles typically mean lower premiums, but you must pay more out-of-pocket before insurance kicks in.

Copay and Coinsurance

Consider the copay and coinsurance for doctor visits, specialist visits, and prescription medications. These costs can add up quickly, so choose a plan with reasonable copays and coinsurance rates.

Paul, a 39-year-old musician, regularly visits doctors and takes prescription medications. He selects a plan with a $20 copay for doctor visits and a 20% coinsurance for prescriptions, balancing his monthly costs and out-of-pocket expenses.

Out-of-Pocket Maximums

Check the out-of-pocket maximums for each plan. This is the most you must pay for covered services in a plan year. Once you reach this limit, your insurance covers 100% of the costs.

Sophie, a 28-year-old engineer, chooses a plan with a $5,000 out-of-pocket maximum. She feels secure knowing that her out-of-pocket costs will be capped, providing financial protection against high medical expenses.

Provider Networks

Ensure your preferred doctors and hospitals are part of the plan's network. Using out-of-network providers can result in higher costs or no coverage at all.

For example, Kevin, a 35-year-old photographer, checks the provider networks for several plans. He selects a plan that includes his preferred primary care physician and specialist, ensuring continuity of care.

Enrolling in a Health Insurance Plan

Once you have chosen a health insurance plan, it is time to enroll. The enrollment process varies depending on whether you get insurance through an employer, the Health Insurance Marketplace (Federal or state exchanges), or directly from an insurance company.

Employer-Sponsored Health Insurance

If you have health insurance through your employer, you typically enroll during the annual open enrollment period. Your employer provides information about the available plans, and you choose the one that best suits your needs.

Betsy, a 27-year-old project manager, reviews her employer's health insurance options. During open enrollment, she selects a PPO plan that offers comprehensive coverage and the flexibility to go to any doctor within the network without a referral.

Health Insurance Marketplace

Suppose you are purchasing health insurance through the Health Insurance Marketplace. To enroll, either join during open enrollment or qualify for the Special Enrollment Period through life events like losing coverage, getting married, losing employment, or having a baby.

Tom, a 31-year-old freelance journalist, uses the Health Insurance Marketplace to compare plans. He enrolls in a PPO plan that fits his budget and provides the coverage he needs.

Private Health Insurance

You can also buy health insurance directly from private insurance companies. This option may offer more flexibility, but comparing plans is essential to ensure you get the best coverage for your needs.

Maria, a 40-year-old small business owner, purchases health insurance directly from a private insurer. She compares several plans and selects a high-deductible health plan (HDHP) with a health savings account (HSA) to balance her premiums and out-of-pocket costs.

Utilizing Your Health Insurance

Once enrolled in a health insurance plan, it's essential to understand how to use it effectively. Adequate health insurance usage includes knowing what is covered, understanding your costs, and maximizing preventive care and other benefits.

Knowing What's Covered

Review your plan's summary of benefits to understand what is covered and any limitations or exclusions. This knowledge will help you avoid unexpected costs and make informed decisions about your care.

Ethan, a 29-year-old college professor, reviews his health insurance plan's summary of benefits. He learns that preventive care, such as annual check-ups and vaccinations, is fully covered, so he schedules his yearly physical to take advantage of this benefit.

Understanding Your Costs

Keep track of your premiums, deductibles, copays, coinsurance, and out-of-pocket maximums. Knowing your costs will help you budget for medical expenses and avoid surprises.

A 34-year-old fashion designer, Angelina tracks her medical expenses throughout the year. She records her deductibles, copays, and coinsurance payments, ensuring she stays within her budget and reaches her out-of-pocket maximum if needed.

Making the Most of Preventive Care

Take advantage of preventive services like vaccinations, screenings, and annual check-ups. Insurance often covers these services fully. Preventive care helps you maintain your health and catch potential issues early, saving you money in the long run.

Lily, a 31-year-old teacher, schedules her annual physical and mammogram as part of her preventive care. These appointments help her stay on top of her health and address any concerns before they become serious issues.

Using In-Network Providers

Whenever possible, use in-network providers to keep your costs lower. Out-of-network providers can result in higher costs or no coverage at all.

Andrew, a 36-year-old architect, ensures he visits in-network doctors and hospitals. He uses his insurance company's online directory to find in-network providers, helping him save money on medical expenses.

Navigating health insurance can be challenging, but understanding the basics and evaluating your needs can help you choose the right plan. You can make informed decisions about your coverage by considering your health status, budget, preferred providers, and the services you use. Remember to review and compare multiple plans, enroll during the appropriate period, and maximize your benefits once you are covered. Be an informed healthcare consumer, optimize your benefits, and maintain a healthy lifestyle.

In the next chapter, we will explore selecting auto insurance, providing you with the knowledge and tools to make confident decisions about your auto insurance coverage.

Chapter Five

Auto and Home Insurance Essentials

"You can't predict, but you can prepare."

– Howard Schultz

A uto and home insurance are crucial components of a comprehensive personal finance plan. They provide financial protection against unexpected events that can cause severe damage or loss to your property. Understanding the essentials of auto and home insurance helps you make informed decisions, ensuring you have the right coverage to protect your assets. This chapter will clarify key concepts using simple, everyday examples to make the topic easy to grasp, enjoyable, and engaging for you and your family.

Why do Auto and Home Insurance Matter?

Auto and home insurance are designed to protect you financially in case of accidents, natural disasters, theft, or other unforeseen events. A home and automobile are important assets that a family could have. It is, therefore, critical that these assets are well protected. Without adequate coverage, the costs of repairing or replacing your vehicle or home can be overwhelming. Insurance helps mitigate these risks, providing peace of mind and financial security. Auto and home insurance protect your vehicle and your home, respectively.

Imagine you are a 35-year-old schoolteacher named Emily. One morning, you wake up to find that a severe storm has damaged your roof. Without home insurance, the cost of repairs could be thousands of dollars. However, with a comprehensive home insurance policy, you can file a claim and have most of the repair costs covered, reducing your financial burden.

Understanding Auto Insurance

Auto insurance is a contract between you and an insurance company that protects you against economic loss in the event of an accident or theft. There are several types of auto insurance coverage, each serving a specific purpose.

Types of Auto Insurance Coverage

Liability Coverage: Liability coverage is required in most states and covers bodily injury and property damage you may cause to others in an accident. It does not cover your own injuries or vehicle damage.

Bodily Injury Liability: This covers medical expenses, lost wages, and legal fees if you are at fault in an accident that injures someone else.

Property Damage Liability: This covers repairing or replacing the other party's vehicle or property damaged in an accident where you are at fault.

John, a 28-year-old marketing manager, is driving to work when he accidentally rear-ends another car. His liability coverage pays for the other driver's medical bills and vehicle repairs, protecting John from significant out-of-pocket expenses.

Collision Coverage

Collision coverage pays for damage to your vehicle resulting from a collision with another car or object, regardless of who is at fault. This coverage is often required if you have a car loan or lease.

Joy, a 30-year-old nurse, swerves to avoid a deer and crashes into a tree. Her collision coverage pays for the repairs to her car, allowing her to get back on the road quickly without a significant financial setback.

Comprehensive Coverage

Comprehensive coverage protects your vehicle against non-collision events like theft, vandalism, natural disasters, and falling objects. Like collision coverage, lenders often require it.

Mike, a 40-year-old Office Manager, wakes up to find out that his car has been stolen. His comprehensive coverage ensures he receives compensation for its value, allowing him to purchase a new vehicle without significant financial strain.

Personal Injury Protection (PIP) or Medical Payments Coverage

PIP or medical payment coverage covers medical expenses for you and your passengers, no matter who caused the accident. PIP may also cover lost wages and other related costs.

Emily, a 35-year-old teacher, and her friend are injured in a car accident. Her PIP coverage helps pay for their medical bills and Emily's lost wages while she recovers, easing the financial impact of the accident on her.

Uninsured/Underinsured Motorist Coverage

Uninsured/underinsured motorist coverage protects you if you are involved in an accident with a driver without insurance or insufficient coverage. It helps pay for medical expenses and vehicle repairs.

Mateo, a 32-year-old house cleaner, is hit by a driver who does not have insurance. His uninsured motorist coverage pays for his medical bills and car repairs, ensuring he does not incur substantial out-of-pocket costs.

Choosing the Right Auto Insurance Policy

Selecting the right auto insurance policy involves evaluating your needs, budget, and the level of coverage required by your state and lender. Here are some steps to help you choose the right policy.

Assess Your Coverage Needs

Consider factors such as your car's value, driving habits, and financial situation. You may want comprehensive and collision coverage if you have a newer or more expensive car. Higher liability limits might be necessary if you frequently drive in high-traffic areas.

For instance, Melody Rodriquez, a 27-year-old lawyer, drives a brand-new car and commutes through busy city streets daily. She opts for comprehensive and collision coverage with higher liability limits to protect her investment in the car and ensure she is adequately covered in case of an accident.

Compare Quotes

Get quotes from multiple insurance companies to find the best rates and coverage options. Use online comparison tools or work with an insurance agent to help you find the right policy.

Jason Peters, a 29-year-old architect, uses an online comparison tool to get quotes from several insurers. By comparing rates and coverage options, he finds a policy that offers the best value for his needs.

Consider Discounts

Many insurance companies offer discounts for safe driving, bundling multiple policies, installing anti-theft devices, and more. Ask about available discounts to lower your premiums.

Megan, a 33-year-old marketing executive, installs an anti-theft device in her car and completes a defensive driving course. She qualifies for multiple discounts, reducing her overall insurance costs.

Review and Update Your Policy Regularly

Your insurance needs may change over time, so it's essential to review your policy annually and adjust as needed. Changes in your vehicle, driving habits, or financial situation can impact your coverage needs. Read and review your policy documents online, or contact your agent for assistance regularly.

Okonkwo, a 38-year-old teacher, reviews his auto insurance policy annually. After paying off his car loan, he drops collision coverage, reducing his premiums and saving money.

Understanding Home Insurance

Home insurance provides financial protection against damage to your home and personal property. It also covers liability for injuries and property damage you or your family members cause to others. There are several types of home insurance coverage, each serving a specific purpose.

Types of Home Insurance Coverage

Dwelling Coverage

Dwelling coverage protects the structure of your home, including the roof, walls, and foundation, against damage from covered perils such as fire, wind, hail, and vandalism.

Uduak, a 40-year-old travel agent, experiences a house fire that damages her kitchen. Her dwelling coverage pays for the repairs, allowing her to restore her home without significant financial hardship.

Other Structures Coverage

This coverage ensures coverage for structures not connected to your home, such as garages, sheds, and fences.

Jody, a 35-year-old engineer, has a detached garage damaged in a storm. His other structures' coverage pays for the repairs, ensuring his property is fully protected.

Personal Property Coverage

Personal property coverage protects your belongings, such as furniture, clothing, electronics, and appliances, against damage or theft. This coverage typically extends to items outside your home, such as those in your car or while traveling.

Bola, a 28-year-old nurse practitioner, has her laptop stolen from her car. Her personal property coverage ensures she receives compensation for the stolen item, allowing her to replace it without financial stress.

Liability Coverage

If someone gets injured on your property or if you accidentally damage someone else's property, liability coverage will provide protection against legal and medical expenses.

Steve, a 42-year-old accountant, had a guest slip and fell on his icy driveway. His liability coverage pays for the guest's medical and legal bills, protecting Steve from significant out-of-pocket costs.

Additional Living Expenses (ALE) Coverage

ALE coverage pays for additional expenses you incur if you temporarily cannot live in your home because of a covered loss, such as restaurant meals, hotel bills, and other living costs.

Ngozi, a 38-year-old pharmacist, must temporarily move out of her home due to a fire. Her ALE coverage pays for her hotel and meal expenses, ensuring she can maintain her standard of living while her house is being repaired.

Choosing the Right Home Insurance Policy

Selecting the right home insurance policy involves evaluating your needs, budget, and the level of coverage required by your mortgage lender. Here are some steps to help you choose the right policy.

Assess Your Coverage Needs

Ensure your insurance coverage is sufficient to rebuild your home and replace belongings in case of a total loss.

Shafiq, a 34-year-old investment banker, calculates the cost of rebuilding his home and the value of his personal property. He chooses a policy with dwelling coverage equal to the cost of rebuilding and personal property coverage sufficient to replace his belongings. Thus, Shafiq is well protected against the total loss of his home because of fire damage.

Compare Quotes

Get quotes from multiple insurance companies to find the best rates and coverage options. Use online comparison tools or work with an insurance agent to help you find the right policy.

A 36-year-old teacher named Bill uses an online comparison tool to get quotes from several insurance companies. By comparing rates and coverage options, he finds a policy that offers the best value for his needs.

Consider Discounts

Many insurance companies offer discounts for bundling policies, installing security systems and sprinkler systems, replacing a roof, and more. Ask about available discounts to lower your premiums.

Samantha, a 40-year-old beautician, installs a security system in her home and replaces her roof. She qualifies for multiple discounts, reducing her overall insurance costs.

Review and Update Your Policy Regularly

Your insurance needs may change over time, so it's essential to review your policy annually and adjust it as needed. Changes in your home's value, personal property, or financial situation can impact your coverage needs.

Hassan, a 42-year-old pilot, reviews his home insurance policy annually. After renovating his home and adding new personal properties, he updates his coverage to ensure he remains fully protected.

Auto and home insurance are essential components of a comprehensive personal finance plan. Understanding the different types of coverage and how to choose the right policies can help you protect your assets and maintain your financial security. You can find the best coverage at affordable rates by assessing your needs, comparing quotes, and taking advantage of discounts. Regularly reviewing and updating your policies ensures you remain adequately protected as your circumstances change.

In the next chapter, we will explore the intricacies of disability insurance, providing you with the knowledge and tools to make confident decisions about your coverage.

Chapter Six

Disability and Long-Term Care Insurance

> "It's not about how much money you make, but how much you keep."
>
> – Robert Kiyosaki

I magine you are living your best life, crushing it at work, and enjoying time with family and friends. Suddenly, an unexpected illness or injury throws a wrench into your plans, and you cannot work for an extended period. How will you pay your bills, mortgage, or support your family without an income? During these challenging times, disability and long-term care insurance come into play. These insurance types provide financial security when life throws you a curve ball. In this chapter, we will explore the essentials of disability and long-term care insurance using simple, everyday examples to clarify the concepts and make them engaging.

Why Disability and Long-Term Care Insurance Matter?

Disability and long-term care insurance protect you from financial hardship due to an illness, injury, or the natural aging process. These policies ensure you have the necessary funds to maintain your lifestyle and care for yourself or your loved ones. Let us dive into each type and see how they can make a difference in your life.

Understanding Disability Insurance

Disability insurance provides income replacement if you cannot work because of a disability. There are two main types of disability insurance: short-term and long-term.

Short-Term Disability Insurance

Short-term disability insurance covers a portion of your income for a brief period, typically three to six months, after a waiting period of a few days to a couple of weeks.

Meet Jane, a 32-year-old middle school bus driver who slips on a wet floor and breaks her leg. The doctor says she will need three months to recover. Jane's short-term disability insurance kicks in after a one-week waiting period, providing her with a portion of her salary while she's unable to work. Jane can focus on her recovery without worrying about her finances.

Long-Term Disability Insurance

Long-term disability insurance kicks in after short-term disability benefits run out, usually after 90 days. Depending on the policy, it can last for several years or until retirement age.

Jackson, a 45-year-old IT manager, is diagnosed with a chronic illness that prevents him from working. After his short-term disability benefits end, his long-term disability insurance begins, providing him with a steady income until he can return to work or reach retirement age. John can cover his expenses and support his family without dipping into his savings.

Own Occupation vs. Any Occupation

When choosing a long-term disability policy, it is essential to understand the difference between "own occupation" and "any occupation" coverage.

- **Own Occupation:** Provides benefits if you cannot perform the duties of your specific job.

- **Any Occupation**: Provides benefits only if you cannot perform the duties of any job for which you are reasonably qualified.

Juliana, a 37-year-old surgeon, develops severe arthritis in her hands and can no longer perform surgeries. With her own occupation policy, Juliana receives benefits because she can no longer perform her specific job as a surgeon. However, with any occupation policy, she might not qualify for benefits if she can still work in another capacity, such as a medical consultant.

How Much Disability Coverage Do You Need?

Determining the right amount of disability coverage depends on your income, monthly expenses, and savings. A good rule of thumb is to aim for a policy that covers 60-70% of your gross income.

Carlos, a 30-year-old software engineer, earns $5,000 a month. He calculates his monthly expenses, including rent, utilities, groceries, and savings, which total $3,500. Carlos chooses a disability policy that provides 70% of his income, or $3,500 a month, ensuring he can maintain his lifestyle if he becomes disabled.

Understanding Long-Term Care Insurance

Long-term care insurance covers the cost of long-term care services, such as nursing homes, assisted living facilities, and in-home care, for individuals who cannot perform daily activities independently due to illness, injury, or aging.

Activities of Daily Living (ADLs)

Long-term care insurance benefits are typically triggered when you cannot perform two or more Activities of Daily Living (ADLs) without assistance. ADLs include:

- Bathing

- Dressing

- Eating

- Transferring (moving from bed to chair)

- Toileting

- Continence

Brody, a 65-year-old retired school superintendent, suffers a stroke that leaves him unable to perform several ADLs. His long-term care insurance policy pays for an in-home caregiver to help him with bathing, dressing, and other daily activities, allowing him to remain in his home rather than move to a nursing facility.

Choosing the Right Long-Term Care Policy

When selecting a long-term care policy, consider the following factors:

Benefit Amount: The maximum daily or monthly amount the policy will pay for care.

Benefit Period: The length of time the policy will pay benefits, typically ranging from two years to a lifetime.

Elimination Period: The waiting period before benefits begin is usually 30-90 days.

Inflation Protection: An option to increase your benefits over time to keep up with rising care costs.

Michelle, a 50-year-old lawyer, purchases a long-term care policy with a $200 daily benefit, a five-year benefit period, and a 90-day elimination period. She also opts for inflation protection to ensure her benefits keep pace with the increasing cost of care. If Michelle needs long-term care in the future, her policy will cover her expenses, providing peace of mind and financial security.

Combining Disability and Long-Term Care Insurance

For comprehensive financial protection, consider combining disability and long-term care insurance. Disability insurance provides income replacement during your working years, while long-term care insurance covers care costs in retirement.

Dorothy, a 40-year-old school principal, has a disability and long-term care insurance. If she becomes disabled and cannot work, her disability insurance will replace her income, allowing her to meet her financial obligations. If Dorothy requires long-term care in retirement, her long-term care policy will cover the costs, ensuring she can afford the care she needs without depleting her savings.

Practical Tips for Busy Professionals and Parents

As busy professionals and parents, finding time to manage your insurance needs can be challenging. Here are some practical tips to help you stay on top of your disability and long-term care insurance.

1. Schedule Annual Reviews

Set aside time each year to review your insurance policies and make any necessary adjustments. Ensure your coverage amounts meet your needs and your beneficiaries are current.

Consider Jude, a 50-year-old electrician who schedules a yearly re-view of his insurance policies every January. He updates his disability and long-term care coverage as his income and family change, ensuring he remains adequately protected.

2. Take Advantage of Employer Benefits

Many employers offer disability and long-term care insurance as part of their benefits package. Review your options and take advantage of em-ployer-sponsored plans, which can be more affordable than purchasing individual policies.

Kofi, a 55-year-old computer systems engineer, enrolls in his compa-ny's long-term care insurance plan during open enrollment. The plan offers comprehensive coverage at a lower cost than individual policies, providing Kofi with peace of mind and financial protection.

3. Work with an Insurance Agent

An insurance agent can help you navigate the complexities of disability and long-term care insurance, ensuring you choose the right policies for your needs. They can also help you find discounts and compare quotes from multiple insurers.

Fatima, a 42-year-old teacher, works with an insurance agent to review her disability and long-term care insurance options. The agent helps her find the best policies and ensures she gets the most value for her money. The insurance company Fatima decides to go with pays the agent's service fee (commission), not Fatima directly.

4. Plan

Consider your long-term financial goals and how disability and long-term care insurance fit into your financial plan. Ensure you have enough coverage to protect your income and assets in case of a disability or need for long-term care.

Joe, a 46-year-old construction worker, includes disability and long-term care insurance in his retirement planning. By securing comprehensive coverage, he ensures his financial future remains stable despite unexpected health issues.

Disability and long-term care insurance are essential components of a comprehensive financial plan. They provide financial protection and peace of mind, ensuring you can maintain your lifestyle and care for yourself or your loved ones in the face of illness, injury, or aging. By understanding the key concepts, assessing your needs, and choosing the right policies, you can secure your financial future and focus on living your best life.

If you found the insights in Chapter 6 and the preceding chapters helpful, I would love to hear your thoughts! Your review helps me and guides others who might benefit from this book. Chapter 8 will dive into Renters and Landlord Insurance as we move forward, covering essential protections whether you're renting your home or managing a property. It's packed with practical advice to ensure you are well-prepared, so stay with me as we explore these important topics.

Chapter Seven

Mid-Book Review Request Page

M ake a Difference with Your Review

Unlock the Power of Generosity

"The best way to find yourself is to lose yourself in the service of others." - Mahatma Gandhi

Taking a moment to help someone else can make your day brighter, your heart lighter, and your life richer. And guess what? You can do that right now, in just a few seconds.

I've got a simple question for you...

Would you help someone you've never met, even if you got nothing in return?

Who is this person, you ask? They're just like you. Maybe they're busy juggling work, family, and life's many responsibilities. Maybe they're trying to figure out how to make their insurance work for them without getting lost in the process.

Our mission with ***How to Make Insurance Work for You: A Personal Finance Guide*** is to make understanding insurance accessible for everyone. Everything I do stems from that mission. But to reach everyone who could benefit from this guide, I need your help.

Here's where you come in. We all know people often judge a book by its cover—and by its reviews. So I'm asking on behalf of someone out there, maybe a parent, a young professional, or a retiree, who's looking for clear answers on how to protect their finances:

Please take a moment to leave a review for this book.

Your review won't cost you a penny; it only takes about 60 seconds. But those 60 seconds can change someone's life. Your review could help...

...one more family feels secure about their future.

...one more young adult understands how to protect what they've worked for.

...one more retiree finds peace of mind.

...one more person takes control of their financial future.

If you want to make a difference, feel good, and help someone in need, all you have to do is...

Leave a review.

It's quick and easy and can genuinely help someone else on their journey. Thank you for being part of this mission!

Please scan the QR code or click the link below to leave your review.

https://www.amazon.com/review/review-your-purchases/?asin=B0DFFV4TDS

If you feel good about helping a faceless parent, a young professional, or a retiree, you are my kind of person. Welcome to the Club. You are one of us.

I'm even more excited to help you make insurance work faster than you can possibly imagine. You'll love the lessons I share in the coming chapters.

Thank you from the bottom of my heart. Now, back to our regularly scheduled reading.

Your biggest fan,

David Okonah

PS - Fun fact: When you provide something of value to another person, it makes you more valuable to them. If you believe this book will help another parent, a young professional, or a retiree —and you believe it will help them—consider sending it their way. Your act of kindness could make a real difference in their journey to financial security.

Chapter Eight

Renters and Landlord Insurance

"**Owning a home is a keystone of wealth... both financial affluence and emotional security.**"

– Suze Orman

Welcome to the world of renters and landlord insurance! Whether you are renting your first apartment or managing several rental properties, understanding the intricacies of these insurance types is crucial. This chapter will break down the essentials of renters and landlord insurance, making it easy to grasp and even enjoyable to read. We will use everyday examples to illustrate key concepts, ensuring you can relate and apply this knowledge effectively.

The Basics of Renters Insurance

Renters insurance, also known as tenant insurance, protects renters from losses from theft, fire, and certain types of water damage. It also covers your personal belongings and provides protection against liability. Landlord's insurance covers the building the tenants dwell in.

Imagine you are Theresa, a 32-year-old home designer living in a cozy apartment. One day, you come home to find that your apartment has been burglarized, and several valuable items are missing. Replacing your stolen belongings would be a significant financial burden without renters' insurance. However, with a good renters insurance policy, you can file a claim and get compensated for your losses, easing the financial stress.

Critical Components of Renters Insurance

Renters insurance covers three components: your belongings, liability, and extra living expenses.

Personal Property Coverage

This coverage protects your personal belongings, such as furniture, electronics, clothing, and more, against covered perils like fire, theft, and vandalism.

Jacob is a 40-year-old realtor with a renter's insurance policy and $30,000 in personal property coverage. When a kitchen fire damages his appliances and furniture, his insurance covers replacing them, saving him thousands of dollars.

Liability Coverage

In situations of injury to a tenant or a visitor on your property, or if you are held responsible for damage to someone else's property, liability coverage protects you.

Abigail, a 35-year-old teacher, rents out her basement apartment. A tenant slips on an icy walkway and decides to sue her for medical expenses. Abigail's landlord insurance policy includes $500,000 in liability coverage, which helps pay for the tenant's medical and legal bills.

Loss of Rental Income Coverage

Loss of rental income coverage, also known as rental income protection, helps compensate for lost rental income if your property becomes uninhabitable due to a covered event.

A 40-year-old truck driver, Bisong, owns a rental property severely damaged by a flood. While the property is being repaired, his landlord's insurance policy covers the lost rental income, ensuring he can still meet his financial obligations.

Determining the Right Amount of Coverage

Choosing the right amount of landlord insurance coverage involves assessing your property's value, potential liability risks, and the rental income you rely on. Here are some steps to help you determine your coverage needs:

Step 1: Evaluate Your Property Value

Determine the replacement cost of your rental property, including the structure and any personal property you provide for tenants.

Drew, an auto mechanic, evaluates the value of his rental property by considering the cost of rebuilding the structure and replacing the appliances and furniture he provides. He ensures his landlord's insurance policy covers the total replacement cost. Drew is smart about protecting his asset.

Step 2: Assess Your Liability Risks

Consider the potential liability risks associated with your rental property. You may need higher liability coverage if you own multiple properties or frequently have tenants and visitors.

Eric, the senior care manager at a nursing home, owns several rental properties. He decides to increase his liability coverage to $1 million to protect himself against potential lawsuits and medical expenses.

Step 3: Calculate Your Rental Income

Estimate your potential loss of rental income if your property becomes uninhabitable. Choose a policy that provides adequate coverage to compensate for this loss.

Francisca, a massage therapist, relies on the rental income from her basement apartment to cover her mortgage payments. She calculates the potential loss of rental income and ensures her landlord insurance policy includes coverage for at least six months of lost rent.

Tips for Managing Renters and Landlord Insurance

Effective management of your renters' and landlords' insurance policies can help you maximize benefits and minimize costs. Here are some practical tips:

1. Regularly Review and Update Your Policies

Life changes, and so do your insurance needs. Review and update your policies regularly to ensure they still provide adequate coverage.

Sarah, a nursing home staff, reviews her renter's insurance policy annually and updates her coverage to reflect any new belongings she owns, or changes in her liability risks.

2. Take Advantage of Discounts

Many insurance companies offer discounts for bundling policies, installing safety features, or maintaining a claims-free history. Ask your insurance provider about available discounts.

The marketing manager, Jones, bundles his auto and renters' insurance policies with the same provider, earning a multi-policy discount that saves him money on both premiums.

3. Implement Safety Measures

Safety measures can reduce damage and liability risk for landlords, lowering insurance premiums. Consider installing smoke detectors, security systems, and regular maintenance checks.

Richard's community manager installs smoke detectors and a security system in his rental property. He also schedules regular maintenance checks to address any potential issues. These measures reduce his insurance premiums if he reports the new additions to his insurance company and provide him peace of mind.

4. Keep Detailed Records

Maintain detailed records of your belongings (for renters) and your property (for landlords). This documentation can help streamline the claims process and ensure you receive fair compensation.

Victoria, a middle school principal, keeps a detailed inventory of her belongings, including furniture, electronics, and jewelry, including photos and receipts. Similarly, Dan, an Uber driver, maintains records of the condition of his rental property and any repairs or upgrades he has made in the last three years. Keeping these records in a safe deposit box or at your local bank is essential for protection against fire or water damage.

Renters and landlord insurance are essential tools for protecting your personal belongings and rental properties. Understanding the critical components of these insurance types, assessing your coverage needs, and implementing practical tips for managing your policies can ensure proper protection. Taking the time to understand and manage your insurance can provide peace of mind and financial security. With the knowledge gained from this chapter, you can confidently navigate the world of renters and landlord insurance.

Just as these insurances provide peace of mind for your living arrangements, navigating Annuity plans is vital to your financial security as you age. In the next chapter, we'll delve into the complexities of Annuity, breaking down the different plans available so you can make informed choices that best suit your financial needs.

Chapter Nine

Understanding Annuities and How They Work for You

"The future belongs to those who prepare for it today."

- Malcolm X.

Introduction to Annuities

Annuities might sound complicated, but at their core, they are simply a way to ensure you have a steady income, especially in retirement. Think of an annuity as a long-term investment with the added benefit of insurance—like setting up a future paycheck for yourself. People buy annuities to help cover their expenses when they are no longer working. If you want to ensure you do not run out of money during retirement, an annuity might be right for you.

Types of Annuities

Let's break down the main types of annuities with some everyday examples:

Immediate vs. Deferred Annuities

Immediate Annuities: Imagine you have just won a prize on a game show. Instead of taking a lump sum, you choose to receive monthly payments starting right away. That is what an immediate annuity does—it turns a lump sum into an immediate income stream.

Deferred Annuities: Now, think about planting a tree. You plant it today, but growing and bearing fruit takes years. A deferred annuity is similar; you invest money now, and it grows over time before starting to pay you an income later, usually when you retire.

Fixed vs. Variable Annuities

Fixed Annuities: Picture a savings account with a guaranteed interest rate. You know exactly how much you will earn each year, no surprises. A fixed annuity works the same way, offering guaranteed payments, making it a safe choice for those who prefer predictability.

Variable Annuities: Imagine investing in the stock market. Your returns are significant in some years; in others, they are lower. A variable annuity lets you invest in different funds, so your payments can vary based on how those investments perform. It's a way to earn more, but with some risk.

Indexed Annuities

Indexed Annuities: Think of an indexed annuity as a hybrid between a fixed and a variable annuity. It's like having a savings account that earns interest based on the performance of a stock market index (like the S&P 500). You can earn more when the market does well, but with a safety net that prevents you from losing money if the market drops.

Annuity Riders

Annuity Riders: Riders are add-ons to your annuity policy like adding extra toppings to your pizza. Do you want extra cheese or a side of garlic bread? That's a rider. In annuities, riders could be options like lifetime withdrawal benefits, ensuring you always have income, or death benefits, protecting your loved ones.

How Annuities Fit Into Your Financial Plan

Annuities can be essential in your financial plan, especially for retirement. Here's how:

Retirement Income

Think of an annuity as a replacement for your paycheck when you retire. Just like you get a regular paycheck while working, an annuity provides regular payments during retirement, helping cover your daily expenses.

Balancing Risk and Reward

Consider your financial plan as a balanced diet. It would help if you had a mix of foods—some carbs, some proteins, and some veggies. Similarly, a mix of fixed annuities (for safety) and variable annuities (for potential growth) can help balance risk and reward in your investment strategy.

Tax Advantages

Imagine growing a garden where the fruits and vegetables are not taxed until you harvest them. An annuity works similarly—your money grows tax-deferred, and you only pay taxes when you start receiving payments.

Ensuring You Don't Outlive Your Savings

Think of an annuity as a safety net at the circus. No matter how high you climb, the net catches you if you fall. An annuity ensures you will not run out of money, providing a financial safety net throughout your retirement.

Choosing the Right Annuity for Your Needs

Selecting the right annuity is about matching your financial goals with the right product. With many annuity products to choose from, there are many factors to consider.

Assessing Your Financial Goals

Consider choosing an annuity, like picking the right shoes for a marathon. You must know your race (retirement goals) to select the right pair (annuity type). Do you need stability (fixed annuity) or growth potential (variable annuity)?

Comparing Fixed, Variable, and Indexed Annuities

It's like choosing between a reliable sedan (fixed annuity), a sporty convertible (variable annuity), or a versatile SUV (indexed annuity). Each has its benefits and is suited to different needs.

Understanding Fees, Costs, and Surrender Charges

Imagine buying a car with a low sticker price but discovering hidden costs like high maintenance fees and penalties for early trade-ins. Annuities can have fees like that, so it is essential to understand the costs before you commit.

Key Questions to Ask Before Purchasing an Annuity

Before buying a house, you should ask about the neighborhood, the schools, and the roof's condition. Similarly, you should ask about the annuity's fees, payout options ,and the insurance company's financial health. Ask about the company's rating with rating agencies like Standard and Poor, Moody, etc. Failure to do these things can ultimately lead to poor annuity-buying decision-making.

Common Pitfalls and How to Avoid Them

Annuities can be complex, and if you are not careful, you can make mistakes. The following are common mistakes to avoid, with everyday examples.

Not Understanding the Surrender Period

Ben, a 60-year-old engineer, purchases an annuity but does not realize it has a 10-year surrender period. When he needs access to his money for an unexpected medical expense, he is hit with a hefty penalty for early withdrawal. Always check the surrender period and associated fees before committing to an annuity. If you anticipate needing access to your funds sooner, choose an annuity with a shorter surrender period or more flexible terms.

Ignoring Fees and Charges

Like buying a concert ticket online and discovering hidden fees at checkout, annuities can have extra costs that reduce your returns. Always read the fine print. For example, a 58-year-old business owner, Titus, purchases an annuity without fully understanding the fees involved. He later realizes that management fees and other charges are eating into his returns, reducing the overall benefit of the annuity. Before buying an annuity, ask for a detailed breakdown of all fees and charges associated with the annuity company. Compare these costs with other investment options to ensure you get a good deal.

Navigating the Complexity of Annuities-Overlooking Inflation Protection

Think of annuities like navigating a new city. Without a map, it's easy to get lost. Understanding the product and getting advice from a financial expert can help guide you through the complexities. : Flora, a 65-year-old retiree, buys an annuity that pays a fixed income, but 10 years into retirement, she finds that her payments do not stretch as far due to rising living costs. Consider annuities with inflation protection or cost-of-living adjustments (COLA). These options may reduce initial payment but will help ensure that your income keeps pace with inflation over time.

Ensuring You Fully Understand the Product Before Buying

It's like reading the instruction manual before assembling a new piece of furniture. Ensure you know what you are getting into, and don't hesitate to ask questions. For instance, Gertrude, a 62-year-old accountant, buys a single-life annuity that stops payments upon her death, leaving her spouse without any income support. Consider a joint-life annuity or a death benefit rider if you have dependents or a spouse. This ensures that your beneficiaries will continue to receive payments after your passing, providing them with financial security.

The Future of Annuities and Retirement Planning

As the world changes, so do the ways we plan for retirement. Here is what is on the horizon for annuities:

Current Trends in the Annuity Market

Think of annuities as evolving from simple landlines to smartphones. Modern annuities, like indexed annuities, are becoming more popular because they offer a mix of security and growth potential. They provide the applicant with the best of both worlds.

Impact of Longer Lifespans on Retirement Planning

Imagine living to 100—your retirement savings must last as long as you do. With people living longer, annuities are becoming more critical for providing income that doesn't run out.

Regulatory Changes and Their Effects on Annuities

Like new traffic laws that change how you drive, regulatory changes can impact how annuities are structured and sold, so staying informed is crucial.

Annuities are powerful tools for securing a steady income during retirement. They come in various types, each suited to different needs and risk levels. Understanding annuities' basics, benefits, and potential pitfalls can help you make informed decisions.

Consider how an annuity could fit into your retirement plan. Assess your goals, compare options, and consult a financial advisor to find the best product for your needs.

Annuities offer a valuable way to ensure long-term financial security. Proper planning and understanding can provide peace of mind and a stable income throughout your retirement. As you look to the future, remember that annuities can be crucial to making your money and insurance work for you.

As you approach retirement, navigating the complexities of healthcare becomes increasingly essential. Medicare, the federal health insurance program for those 65 and older, is crucial to this journey. However, with multiple plans and options, understanding Medicare can feel overwhelming.

In Chapter 10, we will explain the different Medicare insurance plans, and guide you in making the best choice for your health and financial future. Whether you are new to Medicare or reviewing your current coverage, this chapter will help you confidently manage your healthcare needs in retirement.

Chapter Ten

Medicare Insurance Plans

"Planning is bringing the future into the present so that you can do something about it now."

– Alan Lakein

Navigating the world of Medicare can feel like stepping into a maze. With multiple options like Medicare, Medicare Advantage, Medicare Part D, and Medigap plans, it is easy to feel overwhelmed. But do not worry; we are here to guide you through it step by step. This chapter will break down each plan, explain how they work, and help you choose the best options for your needs. We aim to make this process clear and straightforward so you can focus on enjoying your retirement with the peace of mind of knowing your healthcare needs are covered.

Understanding Original Medicare (Part A and Part B)

Let's start with the basics: Original Medicare, which includes Part A and Part B. This is the foundation of Medicare coverage, offering essential healthcare benefits for people 65 and older and certain younger people with disabilities.

Medicare Part A: Hospital Insurance

Medicare Part A helps cover inpatient care in hospitals, skilled nursing facilities, hospice care, and home health care. However, the Part A deductible is not covered in each benefit period (1-60 days) of inpatient stay at the hospital. This deductible varies annually. Check with Medicare for the current year's part A deductible. Most people do not pay a premium for Medicare Part A if they or their spouse paid Medicare taxes for at least forty quarters or ten years while working.

Imagine you are Jim, a 66-year-old retired surveyor. You recently had surgery and needed to stay in the hospital for a few days. Medicare Part A covers most of the costs for your hospital stay, except the Part A deductible, so you can focus on your recovery without worrying about a huge hospital bill.

Medicare Part B: Medical Insurance

Medicare Part B covers outpatient care, doctor's office visits, preventive services, laboratory services, and some home health care. Unlike Part A, Part B requires a monthly premium, which varies based on your income. Medicare Part B also has a deductible that may change yearly, as announced by the Center for Medicare and Medicaid Services. (CMS) Part B generally pays eighty percent of your covered medical expenses.

Gayle, a 68-year-old former chef, visits her doctor regularly for check-ups and manages her diabetes. Medicare Part B helps cover most of the cost of her doctor visits, lab tests, and preventive services like flu shots, making it easier for her to stay on top of her health.

Medicare Advantage Plans (Part C)

Medicare Advantage, also known as Part C, is a private insurance company-sponsored alternative to Original Medicare. These private companies have contracts with the Federal government through the Center for Medicare and Medicaid Services(CMS) that are renewed annually. CMS highly regulates them to ensure Medicare beneficiaries are not taken advantage of. These comprehensive plans offer all the benefits of Medicare Part A and Part B. Some include prescription drug coverage and extra benefits such as vision, dental, home-delivered meals, hearing, and wellness programs, while others provide extra benefits but no prescription drug coverage.

How Medicare Advantage Works

The Center for Medicare and Medicaid Services (CMS) requires Medicare Advantage plans to offer at least the same coverage as Original Medicare, but they often include extra benefits. These plans usually operate like HMOs or PPOs, where you may need to choose a primary care doctor and get referrals to see specialists.

Edward, a 70-year-old retired engineer, likes to travel. He chooses a Medicare Advantage plan with worldwide emergency coverage and dental benefits, which Original Medicare doesn't cover. This plan gives him the flexibility and peace of mind to enjoy his retirement.

Pros and Cons of Medicare Advantage

Pros: Extra benefits, often lower out-of-pocket costs, and a one-stop shop for coverage (hospital, medical, and drug coverage in one plan).

Cons: Limited provider networks, specialist visits may require referrals, and out-of-network care might cause higher costs.

Sally, a 65-year-old retired librarian, likes the convenience of having all her healthcare needs covered under one plan. However, her favorite specialist is not in her Medicare Advantage plan's network, so she will have to pay more out of pocket to continue seeing that doctor; the doctor may choose not to see her, or she could find another doctor in the network.

Medicare Part D: Prescription Drug Coverage

Medicare Part D provides prescription drug coverage, which is not included in Original Medicare. You can add Part D to your Medicare coverage by enrolling in a stand-alone prescription drug plan (PDP) or by choosing a Medicare Advantage plan that includes prescription drug coverage.

How Medicare Part D Works

Private insurance companies offer Part D plans that cover a list of drugs known as a formulary. These plans have different costs and coverage rules, so it is essential to choose one that covers the medications you take regularly. Some Part D plans have deductibles, and some do not. Depending on your medication's levels or tiers, you may pay higher or lower copayments for your prescription drugs. Part D Formulary tiers 1 and 2 medications are usually less expensive than those in tiers 3 -5.

Barbara, a 69-year-old retired accountant, takes several medications for high blood pressure and cholesterol. She enrolls in a Medicare Part D plan that covers her prescriptions at an affordable cost, allowing her to manage her health without breaking the bank.

Choosing a Part D Plan

When selecting a Part D plan, consider the following:

Formulary: Does the plan cover the drugs you take?

Costs: What are the premiums, deductibles, copayments, and coinsurance?

Pharmacy Network: Can you use your preferred pharmacy?

John, a 67-year-old former professor, researches Part D and plans to find one that covers his specific medications with the lowest out-of-pocket costs. To avoid inconvenience, he also checks that his local pharmacy is in the plan's network to avoid any surprises.

Medigap Plans: Supplemental Insurance

Medigap, also known as Medicare Supplement Insurance, helps cover the out-of-pocket costs that Original Medicare does not pay, such as copayments, coinsurance, and deductibles. Private insurance companies offer Medigap plans designed to work alongside Original Medicare.

How Medigap Plans Work

Medigap plans are standardized, offering the same essential benefits regardless of which insurance company you buy from. There are different Medigap plans, labeled A through N, each offering a different level of coverage. Medigap plans do not include prescription drugs. Medicare beneficiaries must enroll in a Medicare Part D stand-alone plan to have prescription drug benefits.

Ellen, a 70-year-old retired school principal, chose Medigap Plan G because it covers all her Medicare Part A deductible, Part B coinsurance, and hospital costs. Thus, she does not have to worry about unexpected medical bills. This extra coverage gives her peace of mind, knowing she is protected against high healthcare costs.

Choosing a Medigap Plan

When selecting a Medigap plan, consider your healthcare needs, budget, and desired coverage. Medigap plans can be more expensive than Medicare Advantage plans, but they offer broader access to healthcare providers.

Bolton, a 68-year-old retired lawyer, values flexibility in his healthcare. He chooses a Medigap plan that allows him to see any doctor or specialist who accepts Medicare without needing referrals or worrying about network restrictions. However, to have a prescription drug benefit, he must enroll in a stand-alone Medicare Part D plan and pay an additional premium.

Key Differences Between Medicare Advantage and Medigap

While Medicare Advantage and Medigap offer ways to manage your healthcare costs, they work differently. Here's a comparison to help you understand which might be better for your needs:

Coverage: Medicare Advantage includes all-in-one coverage for hospital, medical, extra benefits, and often drug benefits. Medigap or Medicare supplements cover the gaps in the Original Medicare, covering out-of-pocket costs with no prescription drugs.

Provider Access: Medicare Advantage may restrict you to a network of doctors and hospitals. Medigap allows you to see any provider who accepts Medicare.

Cost: Medicare Advantage often has lower premiums but higher out-of-pocket costs. Medigap typically has higher premiums but can reduce overall expenses by covering more costs.

Flexibility: Medicare Advantage plans may change their benefits and costs each year. Medigap plans are standardized and offer consistent coverage.

Sonia, a 69-year-old retired social worker, considers both Medicare Part C and Medigap options. She appreciates the simplicity of Medicare Advantage but decides on Medigap for the flexibility to see any doctor, especially since she travels frequently to visit her grandchildren across the country.

Making the Right Choice for You

Choosing between Original Medicare, Medicare Advantage, Part D, and Medigap depends on your health needs, lifestyle, and financial situation. It's essential to evaluate all your options and consider factors such as:

- Your Health Needs: Do you need regular medical care, prescription drugs, or specialty services?

- Your Budget: What can you afford in premiums, deductibles, coinsurance, and out-of-pocket costs?

- Your Lifestyle: Do you travel frequently or prefer flexibility in choosing healthcare providers?

- Your Peace of Mind: Do you prefer comprehensive coverage that minimizes surprise costs, or are you comfortable with more cost-sharing to lower premiums?

Jim and Carol, both 67 and recently retired, sit together to evaluate their healthcare options. Jim, who has a few chronic conditions, opts for Medigap and Part D to ensure he has comprehensive coverage with predictable costs. Carol, who is generally healthy and likes the simplicity of one plan, chooses Medicare Advantage for its extra benefits like prescription, dental, hearing, meal delivery, and vision benefits.

Navigating Medicare can seem complex, but understanding your options—Original Medicare, Medicare Advantage, Part D, and Medigap—helps you make informed decisions that suit your health and financial needs. Take the time to review each option, compare plans, and consider what works best for your lifestyle and budget. Contact your local State Health Insurance Assistance Programs (SHIPs) or qualified Medicare expert for help.

Remember, the goal is to ensure you have healthcare coverage so you can enjoy your retirement with confidence and peace of mind. By choosing the right Medicare plans, you can focus on living life to the fullest, knowing your healthcare needs are covered.

In the next chapter, we will explore strategies for maximizing your insurance benefits while minimizing costs, helping you get the most out of your coverage. Whether managing multiple Medicare plans or considering a Medigap policy, these tips will help you make the most of your healthcare dollars.

Chapter Eleven

Maximizing Insurance Benefits and Minimizing Costs

"Beware of little expenses; a small leak will sink a great ship."

– Benjamin Franklin

Navigating the insurance world can feel like solving a never-ending puzzle. With premiums, deductibles, coverage limits, and endless fine print, it is easy to get overwhelmed. However, understanding how to maximize your benefits while minimizing costs is crucial for protecting your financial well-being. This chapter will explore practical strategies for getting the most out of your insurance policies without breaking the bank.

Understanding Your Insurance Policies

The first step in maximizing your benefits and minimizing costs is fully understanding your insurance policies. Policy understanding means knowing what is covered, what is not, and how to maximize your coverage. Whether the policy is life, health, auto, home, or disability insurance, there are critical elements to maximizing benefits and minimizing costs.

Read Your Policy Documents

While it may not be the most thrilling reading material, taking the time to read your policy documents can save you a lot of headaches later. Pay attention to the coverage details, exclusions, and any applicable conditions.

Imagine you are Bintu, a 34-year-old homemaker, and you decide to skip reading the fine print of your auto insurance policy. Later, you discover that your policy does not cover rental cars, leaving you stranded while your vehicle is in the shop. By reading your policy documents, you could have avoided this surprise and chosen a plan that covers car rental that better suits your needs.

Ask Questions

If you need clarification on your policy, ask your insurance agent or call the insurance company. Ensure that you have the policy number ready when you make the call. It is better to ask questions now than to be caught off guard later.

A 40-year-old business analyst, Donald, calls his insurance agent to ask about the difference between collision and comprehensive coverage. His agent explains that collision covers accidents with other vehicles or objects, while comprehensive covers non-collision events like theft or natural disasters. With this information, Donald feels more confident in his coverage choices.

Bundling Policies

One of the easiest ways to save money on insurance is by bundling multiple policies with the same provider. Many insurance companies offer discounts for bundling, which can significantly reduce your overall costs.

Judy, a 28-year-old traveling nurse, has both auto and renters' insurance. By bundling these policies with the same insurer, she receives a 15% discount on both, saving her hundreds of dollars each year. Plus, she enjoys the convenience of having all her policies managed in one place.

Increasing Deductibles

Raising your deductibles is another effective way to lower your insurance premiums. A higher deductible means you will pay more out-of-pocket in case of a claim, but your monthly premiums will be lower.

Alejandra, a 32-year-old business owner, increases her auto insurance deductible from $500 to $1,000, reducing her monthly premium by $30. She keeps the extra savings in an emergency fund to cover the higher deductible if needed.

Taking Advantage of Discounts

Insurance companies offer various discounts that can help you save money. You can get discounts for being a safe driver, having multiple policies, being a good student, and installing safety devices.

Pablo, a 29-year-old software developer, installs a security system in his home and notifies his insurance company. He qualifies for a discount on his homeowner's insurance, reducing his premium by 10%. Pablo also completes a defensive driving course, earning a safe driver discount on his auto insurance.

Maintaining a Good Credit Score

Many insurance companies use your credit score to determine your premiums. Keeping a good credit score can help you qualify for lower rates.

Many insurance companies consider your credit score when determining your premiums. Maintaining a good credit score can help you qualify for lower rates.

Paula, a 45-year-old social worker, regularly checks her credit report and pays her bills on time. Her excellent credit score helps her secure lower auto and homeowners' insurance premiums.

Reviewing and Updating Your Coverage

Your insurance needs can change, so reviewing and updating your coverage is essential. This policy review ensures you have the right amount of protection and are not paying for coverage you no longer need.

Malik, a 42-year-old police officer, reviews his auto insurance policy each year. After paying off his car loan, he drops collision coverage, reducing his premium. Malik also reviews his homeowners' insurance after renovating his home, ensuring his coverage reflects the increased value. This protects Malik against being underinsured for his property.

Maximizing Health Insurance Benefits

Health insurance is a critical part of your financial plan, and understanding how to maximize your benefits can save you a lot of money on medical expenses.

Use In-Network Providers

In-network providers have agreements with your insurance company to provide services at discounted rates. Using in-network providers can significantly reduce your out-of-pocket costs.

Antonia, a 30-year-old marketing executive, checks her health insurance provider's website to find an in-network specialist for her annual check-up. By staying in-network, she avoids higher costs and unexpected bills.

Take Advantage of Preventive Care

Many health insurance plans cover preventive care services, such as annual check-ups, vaccinations, and screenings, at no additional cost. Utilizing these services can help you stay healthy and catch potential issues early.

Brian, a 38-year-old engineer, schedules his annual physical and flu shot through his health insurance plan. These preventive services are fully covered, helping Michael stay healthy and avoid more costly medical issues.

Understand Your Prescription Coverage

Knowing which medications are covered under your plan's formulary and whether there are generic alternatives can save you money on prescriptions.

Veronica, a 34-year-old teacher, needs a prescription for a chronic condition. She checks her health insurance plan's formulary and finds a generic alternative to her medication. By choosing the generic option, Veronica saves money on her monthly prescription costs.

Maximizing Auto Insurance Benefits

Auto insurance protects you financially in accidents, theft, or other vehicle-related incidents. Here are some tips to maximize your auto insurance benefits:

Drive Safely

Maintaining a clean driving record can help you qualify for safe driver discounts and keep your premiums low.

Erica, a 28-year-old nurse, follows traffic laws and practices defensive driving. Her clean driving record earns her a safe driver discount, reducing her auto insurance premium.

Consider Usage-Based Insurance

Some insurance companies offer usage-based insurance programs that use telematics devices to track your driving habits. If you are a safe driver, you could save money on your premiums.

Mark, a 40-year-old marketing manager, enrolls in a usage-based insurance program. The telematics device tracks his safe driving habits, and Mark earns a discount on his auto insurance for being a responsible driver.

Take Advantage of Rental Car Coverage

If your policy includes rental car coverage, use it when your vehicle is in the shop for repairs after an accident. This benefit can save you money on rental car costs.

For example, Judy, a 35-year-substitute teacher, has rental car coverage on her auto insurance policy. When her car is in the shop after an accident, her insurance pays for a rental car, allowing her to get around without additional expenses.

Maximizing Home Insurance Benefits

Home insurance protects your home and belongings from damage, theft, and other risks. Here are some tips to maximize your home insurance benefits:

Maintain Your Home

Regular maintenance and repairs can prevent damage and reduce the likelihood of filing a claim. Some insurance companies offer discounts for home improvements that reduce risk, such as installing a new roof or upgrading plumbing.

Jones, a 42-year-old project manager, replaces his old, less durable roof with a new one. He notifies his insurance company and qualifies for a discount on his homeowners' insurance. Regular maintenance also helps Jones avoid costly repairs and potential claims.

Keep an Inventory of Your Personal Property

Maintaining an up-to-date inventory of your belongings, such as jewelry, books, artwork, furniture, musical instruments, etc., can help you file a claim quickly and accurately if your home is damaged or burglarized.

Mara, a 30-year-old sports enthusiast, uses a smartphone app to inventory her belongings, including her handbags, books, and media equipment, along with photos and descriptions. When her home is burglarized, she provides the inventory to her insurance company, speeding up the claims process and ensuring she receives total compensation for her losses.

Take Advantage of Additional Living Expenses (ALE) Coverage

ALE coverage can help pay for temporary housing and other living expenses if your home becomes uninhabitable due to a covered loss. Be sure to use this benefit if you need it.

Joel, a 38-year-old sales associate, must leave his home temporarily after a fire. His ALE coverage pays for his hotel stay and additional living expenses, allowing him to maintain his standard of living while his house is being repaired.

Shopping Around for the Best Rates

One of the best ways to minimize insurance costs is to shop around and compare quotes from multiple insurers. Insurance companies offer different rates and discounts, so finding the best deal is worth it.

Vita, a 34-year-old teacher, uses an online comparison tool to get quotes from several insurance companies. By comparing rates and coverage options, she finds a policy that offers the best value for her needs and saves money on her premiums.

Understanding and Using Policy Riders

Policy riders, or endorsements, allow you to customize your insurance coverage to better suit your needs. Understanding and using these riders can help maximize your benefits and ensure proper protection.

Common Auto Insurance Riders

Roadside Assistance: Covers towing, flat tire changes, and roadside services.

Rental Reimbursement: Pays for a rental car while your vehicle is being repaired after a covered loss.

Gap Insurance: This covers the difference between your car's actual cash value and the remaining loan balance if your vehicle is totaled.

Erica, a 28-year-old customer service representative, adds a roadside assistance rider to her auto insurance policy. When she gets a flat tire on the way to work, she calls her insurer, and they send help to change the tire, saving her time and money.

Common Home Insurance Riders

- **Scheduled Personal Property:** Provides additional coverage for valuable items like jewelry, art, and electronics.

- **Water Backup Coverage:** This covers damage caused by water backing up from sewers or drains.

- **Identity Theft Protection**: Covers expenses related to restoring your identity if it's stolen.

Eli, a 40-year-old marketing manager, adds a scheduled personal property rider to his home insurance policy to cover his expensive camera equipment. When his camera is stolen, the rider ensures he receives total compensation for the loss.

Leveraging Health Savings Accounts (HSAs)

If you have a high-deductible health plan (HDHP), you can use a Health Savings Account (HSA) to save pre-tax dollars for medical expenses. HSAs offer triple tax benefits: contributions are tax-deductible, earnings grow tax-free, and withdrawals for qualified medical expenses are tax-free.

Petra, a 35-year event planner, contributes to an HSA alongside her HDHP. She uses the account to pay for medical expenses like doctor visits and prescriptions. The tax advantages help Petra save money, and she can invest unused funds for future healthcare costs.

Maximizing your insurance benefits while minimizing costs is vital to financial planning. By understanding your policies, taking advantage of discounts, and regularly reviewing your coverage, you can get the best value for your money. Shopping around for the best rates, using policy riders, and leveraging health savings accounts can further enhance your financial protection and savings.

In the next chapter, we will delve into the process of filing insurance claims and dealing with denials, providing you with the knowledge and tools to handle claims efficiently and effectively.

Chapter Twelve

Navigating Claims and Avoiding Pitfalls

"The most important thing in communication is hearing what isn't said."

– Peter Drucker

Filing an insurance claim can be as thrilling as watching paint dry. Yet, it is essential to manage your insurance coverage and ensure you get the financial protection you deserve. Navigating the claims process efficiently and avoiding common pitfalls can significantly affect the outcome. This chapter will provide practical tips and simple, everyday examples to help you effectively manage claims. Let us dive into insurance claims and make it as engaging and straightforward as possible.

Understanding the Claims Process

The first step in navigating insurance claims is understanding the process. While the specifics can vary depending on the type of insurance and the insurer, the general steps are usually quite similar.

Step 1: Reporting the Claim

The claims process begins when you report the Incident to your insurance company. The Incident could be a car accident, a burst pipe in your home, a medical emergency, or death. Timely reporting is crucial, as delays can complicate the process.

Imagine you are Amy, a 60-year-old bus driver, and you discover a pipe bursting in your home, causing water damage. You promptly call your home insurance company to report the Incident, providing them with the necessary details and starting the claims process.

Step 2: Documentation and Evidence

Once you have reported the claim, you must document the damage or loss. The documentation includes taking photos, gathering receipts, and noting relevant details. The more thorough your documentation, the smoother the process will be.

Jake, a 35-year-old software developer, is involved in a minor car accident. He takes photos of the damage, exchanges information with the other driver, and writes down the details of the Incident. Jake's thorough documentation helps his insurance company process the claim quickly.

Step 3: Working with an Adjuster

An insurance adjuster will be assigned to your claim. Their job is to assess the damage or loss and determine the amount your insurance company will pay. Be prepared to provide them with all the documentation and evidence you have gathered.

Ann, a 45-year-old Nurse manager, is filing a claim for storm damage to her roof. An adjuster visits her home to inspect the damage. Ann provides the adjuster with photos and receipts for previous roof repairs, helping the adjuster make an accurate assessment.

Step 4: Settlement and Payment

After the adjuster has evaluated your claim, the insurance company will make a settlement offer. If you agree with the offer, they will issue a payment to cover the damages or losses. If you disagree, you may need to negotiate or provide additional information.

Basil, a 50-year-old data analyst, files a claim for a stolen laptop. The insurance company offers a settlement that Basil feels is too low. He provides additional documentation showing the laptop's value and negotiates a higher settlement.

Common Pitfalls to Avoid

Filing an insurance claim can be straightforward, but common pitfalls can trip you up. Here is how to avoid them:

Pitfall 1: Delaying the Claim

Waiting too long to report a claim can lead to complications or even denial. Always report incidents as soon as possible.

Patricia, a 35-year-old stay-at-home mom, hesitates to report a minor fender bender because she thinks the damage is not severe. Two weeks later, she realizes the repair costs are higher than expected. By then, the delay complicates her claim process.

Pitfall 2: Inadequate Documentation

Please properly document the damage or loss to avoid a lower settlement or denial. Always take photos, gather receipts, and note details immediately after the Incident.

Ibrahim, a 38-year-old Dental hygienist, experienced a burglary at his home but must thoroughly document the missing items. When he files the claim, the lack of documentation makes it difficult for the insurance company to verify the losses, leading to a reduced settlement.

Pitfall 3: Accepting the First Offer

The insurance company's first settlement offer might sometimes be fair. Negotiating or providing additional evidence is okay if you believe the offer is too low.

Lydia, a 42-year-old hairdresser, receives a low settlement offer for water damage in her basement. She gathers more documentation, including repair estimates, and negotiates with the insurance company for a fairer settlement.

Pitfall 4: Not Understanding Your Policy

Not fully understanding your policy can lead to unpleasant surprises when filing a claim. Know your coverage limits, exclusions, and deductibles.

Kwame, a 45-year-old engineer, files a claim for flood damage only to learn that his homeowners' insurance does not cover flooding. Kwame realizes he must purchase a separate flood insurance policy for future protection.

Maximizing Your Claim

To get the most out of your insurance claim, follow these strategies:

Be Thorough and Honest

Provide complete and accurate information when filing your claim. Misrepresenting facts can lead to denial or even cancellation of your policy.

Anna, a 32-year-old retail store manager, filed a claim for a stolen bicycle. She provided honest and detailed information about the Incident, including the exact date and location of the theft. Her thoroughness ensured a smooth claims process, and her claim was paid in a timely manner.

Keep a Claims Diary

Maintain a diary of all interactions with your insurance company, including dates, names, claim numbers, policy numbers, and details of conversations. This record can help you keep track of the process and provide a reference if issues arise.

Tama, a 40-year-old journalist, keeps a diary of all phone calls and emails about his auto insurance claim. He refers to it to resolve any discrepancies quickly.

Seek Professional Help if Needed.

If your claim is complex or you need help with the insurance company, consider hiring a public adjuster or attorney to help you navigate the process.

Fiafia, a 50-year-old Medical assistant, hires a public adjuster to help with her complicated homeowners' insurance claim after a severe storm. The adjuster's expertise helps Fiafia secure a fair settlement.

Navigating Specific Types of Claims

Different types of insurance claims have unique considerations. Here is how to manage some common scenarios:

Auto Insurance Claims

Auto insurance claims often involve accidents, theft, or damage to your vehicle. Here are some tips for navigating these claims:

- Report the Incident: Contact your insurance company immediately after an accident or theft.

- Document the Scene: Take photos, gather witness information, and note the details of the Incident.

- Get a Police Report: For accidents or theft, a police report can support your claim.

Peni, a 35-year-old software developer, was involved in a minor car accident. He took photos, exchanged information with the other driver, and filed a police report. Peni's thorough documentation helped his insurance company process the claim quickly.

Home Insurance Claims

Home insurance claims can involve damage from natural disasters, theft, or accidents. Here are some tips for navigating these claims:

Mitigate Further Damage: Prevent additional damage, such as covering a broken window or drying out water damage.

Document Everything: Take photos, keep receipts for repairs, and note all details.

Work with Contractors: Obtain repair estimates from reputable contractors to support your claim.

Mele, a 45-year-old Medical Doctor, experiences a burst pipe in her home. She turns off the water, dries out the affected area, and takes photos of the damage. Mele gets repair estimates and submits them to her insurance company, ensuring a smooth claims process.

Health Insurance Claims

Health insurance claims often involve medical treatments, hospital stays, or prescription medications. Here are some tips for navigating these claims:

- Know Your Coverage: Understand your policy's coverage, including deductibles, co-payments, and exclusions.

- Keep Detailed Records: Maintain records of medical bills, prescriptions, and communications with healthcare providers.

- Appeal Denied Claims: Do not hesitate to appeal if a claim is denied. Provide additional documentation and explanations as needed.

Vai, a 42-year-old teacher, files a claim for a medical procedure. When the claim is initially denied, she reviews her policy, gathers additional medical records, and submits an appeal. Vai's persistence pays off, and the claim is approved.

Life Insurance Claims

Life insurance is a crucial safety net for your loved ones, providing financial security in the event of your passing. When filing a claim, it is essential to understand the process and avoid unnecessary delays.

1. Notify the Insurance Company: The first step is for the beneficiary or a family member to inform the life insurance company of the policyholder's death. A copy of the death certificate is needed to initiate the claim.

2. Complete the Claim Form: The insurance company will provide a claim form the beneficiary must fill out. Ensure all details are accurate to avoid delays.

3. Submit Required Documentation: You must submit the death certificate and, in some cases, the original policy document and the claim form. Keep copies of everything you submit.

Imagine you are Clarissa, a 40-year-old store cashier. After the unexpected passing of your spouse, you need to file a claim on his life insurance policy. You promptly notify the insurance company, gather the necessary documents, and carefully fill out the claim form. Within a few weeks, the claim is processed, and you receive the policy benefits less any loan amount if any, helping you manage the financial challenges ahead.

Disability Income Insurance Claims

Disability income insurance is an essential safety net that provides financial support if you are unable to work due to illness or injury. Filing a disability income insurance claim requires careful attention to detail and prompt action. Here is a step-by-step guide to help you through the process:

- Review Your Policy: Before filing a claim, review your disability income insurance policy. Understand the coverage details, including the definition of disability, the elimination period (the waiting period before benefits begin), and the benefit duration.

- Notify Your Employer and Insurance Provider: As soon as you become aware that you cannot work due to a disability, inform your employer and insurance provider. They will guide you through the initial steps of the claims process.

- Gather Medical Documentation: You will need to provide comprehensive medical documentation to support your claim. This record includes statements from your doctor detailing your condition, treatment plans, and how your disability prevents you from performing your job.

- Complete the Claim Form: Your insurance provider will give you a claim form to fill out. This form will require information about your medical condition, job duties, and how your disability affects your ability to work. Be thorough and accurate to avoid delays.

- Submit Supporting Documents: Along with the claim form, you will need to submit additional documentation such as your medical records, proof of income, and possibly a statement from your employer verifying your job duties and the impact of your disability.

- Follow Up Regularly: Contact your insurance provider regularly after submitting your claim. Frequent contact with the claim department ensures your claim is being processed and allows you to promptly address any additional requests for information.

Alesana, a 45-year-old construction worker, must file a claim after a severe car accident leaves him unable to work. He carefully reviews his policy to understand his coverage and elimination period. Alesana gathers all necessary medical records, completes the claim form accurately, and submits everything to his insurance provider. He regularly checks in with his provider to ensure the claim is progressing, and within a few weeks, he begins receiving his disability benefits.

Long-Term Care Insurance Claims

Long-term care insurance helps cover care costs when someone cannot perform basic daily activities independently. Filing a claim for long-term care can be more complex, so it is essential to follow these steps closely.

1. Understand the Policy: Before filing a claim, review the policy to understand what is covered, including the types of care and any waiting periods.

2. Notify the Insurance Company: Inform the insurance company when long-term care is needed. They will guide you through the specific requirements for filing a claim.

3. Provide Medical Documentation: You will likely need documentation from a healthcare provider confirming the need for long-term care and outlining the level of assistance required.

4. Coordinate with Care Providers: Work closely with the care facility or provider to ensure they meet the policy's criteria. This ensures that the insurance will cover the costs.

Raj, a 55-year-old banker, must file a claim for his aging mother's long-term care insurance. He reviews the policy and works with her doctor to gather the necessary medical documentation. He then contacts the insurance company and follows their instructions for filing the claim. By staying organized, Raj ensures his mother receives her care without financial strain.

Handling Claim Denials

Receiving a claim denial can be frustrating, but it's not the end of the road. Here is how to manage denials effectively:

Understand the Reason

Review the denial letter carefully to understand why the claim was denied. It could be due to missing information, coverage issues, or errors.

Kenji, a 50-year-old physician, receives a denial letter for his water damage claim. The letter states that the damage is considered long-term and not covered. Kenji reviews the details and realizes he needs more evidence to prove the damage was sudden.

Gather Additional Evidence

If the denial is due to missing information or documentation, gather the necessary evidence and resubmit the claim.

Martha, a 30-year-old nurse, had her car accident claim denied due to insufficient evidence. She gathered additional photos and witness statements and resubmitted the claim, which was approved.

File an Appeal

If you believe the denial is unjustified, file an appeal with your insurance company. Provide a detailed explanation and any additional documentation that supports your case.

Hyun, a 38-year-old software developer, appealed a denial for his storm damage claim. He submitted a detailed letter explaining the damage, including additional photos and repair estimates. Hyun's appeal was successful, and the claim was approved.

Seek External Help

If the appeal is unsuccessful, seek help from a public adjuster, attorney, or your state's insurance department.

Alexandria, a 42-year-old photographer, hires a public adjuster to help with her denied homeowner's insurance claim. The adjuster's expertise helps Alexandria successfully appeal the denial and secure a fair settlement.

Tips for Busy Professionals and Parents

Balancing work and family and managing insurance claims can be challenging. Here are some tips to help busy professionals and parents navigate the claims process efficiently:

1. Create a Claims Checklist

Develop a checklist of steps to take when filing a claim, including reporting the Incident, documenting the damage, and gathering necessary information. This checklist can help you stay organized and complete all essential steps.

Minho, a 35-year-old bartender, creates a checklist for auto insurance claims. When involved in a minor accident, the checklist helps him quickly and efficiently document the Incident and report it to his insurance company.

2. Set Aside Time for Claims

Dedicate specific times each week to managing your insurance claims. This time can help you stay on the process and avoid delays.

A 45-year-old graphic designer, Missy sets aside an hour every Sunday to review and manage her insurance claims. This routine helps her stay organized and ensures her claims are processed smoothly.

3. Use Technology

Take advantage of online tools and apps offered by your insurance company to file and track claims. These tools can simplify the process and save you time.

Trent, a 38-year-old data analyst, uses his insurance company's mobile app to file a claim for storm damage. The app allows him to upload photos, track the status of his claim, and communicate with his adjuster, making the process more efficient.

Navigating insurance claims can be manageable. You can manage claims efficiently and effectively by understanding the process, avoiding common pitfalls, and following practical tips. When dealing with auto, home, or health insurance claims, being thorough, organized, and proactive in claim processing can help you get the financial protection you deserve.

In the next chapter, we will explore reviewing and updating your insurance policies to ensure you have the right coverage at the best rates.

Chapter Thirteen

Reviewing and Updating Your Policies

"Continuous improvement is better than delayed perfection."

– Mark Twain

L ife is full of changes. You get married, have kids, buy a home, switch jobs, or even start a side hustle. These milestones can significantly impact your insurance needs. Regularly reviewing and updating your insurance policies ensures you remain adequately protected without overpaying. This chapter will guide you through reviewing and updating your policies, using simple and everyday examples to make the task less daunting and, dare we say, even enjoyable.

Why Reviewing Your Policies is Important

Insurance is not a "set it and forget it" aspect of your financial plan. Regular reviews ensure your coverage keeps pace with your life changes and evolving risks. Here are some key reasons why you should make this a regular practice:

1. Life Changes: Major life events such as marriage, the birth of a child, or buying a new home can affect your insurance needs.

2. Policy Adjustments: You might need to adjust your coverage over time to avoid being underinsured or overinsured.

3. Discounts and Savings: Regular reviews can help you identify new discounts and savings opportunities.

4. Keeping Up with Inflation: The cost of replacing your assets can increase as inflation increases, so your coverage should reflect current values.

Imagine you are Aisha, a 35-year-old travel agent who recently welcomed a new baby. If something happens to you, your current life insurance policy might not provide enough coverage to secure your family's future. Reviewing and updating your policy can increase coverage to meet your growing family's needs.

When to Review Your Policies

While it is an excellent practice to review your policies annually, certain life events should prompt an immediate review:
1. Marriage or Divorce
2. Birth or Adoption of a Child
3. Buying or Selling a Home
4. Starting or Changing Jobs
5. Major Home Renovations
6. Purchasing High-Value Items
7. Changes in Health

Wei, a 40-year-old entrepreneur, gets promoted and moves into a bigger house. This momentous change in his financial and living situation prompts him to review his homeowners and life insurance policies to ensure he has adequate coverage.

How to Review Your Insurance Policies

Reviewing your insurance policies can be a simple task. Follow these steps to make the process smooth and efficient:

Step 1: Gather Your Policy Documents

Start by gathering all your insurance policy documents. These policy documents include auto, home, health, life, and any other types of insurance you have.

Hilary, a 32-year-old seamstress, creates a folder on her computer to store digital copies of her insurance policies. She also keeps a physical binder with printed copies, making it easy to review her coverage annually.

Step 2: Check Your Coverage Limits

Review each policy's coverage limits to ensure they still meet your needs. Pay attention to your liability limits, property coverage, and specific endorsements or riders.

A 38-year-old plumber, Casey reviews his auto insurance policy and realizes his liability coverage is lower than he would like. He decides to increase his coverage limits to provide better financial protection in case of an accident.

Step 3: Evaluate Deductibles

Your deductible is paid out of pocket before your insurance kicks in. Make sure your deductible is set at a level you can comfortably afford.

Rita, a 45-year-old web designer, reviews her homeowner's insurance policy and decides to increase her deductible from $500 to $1,000. This adjustment lowers her premium, saving her money each month.

Step 4: Update Personal Information

Ensure all personal information on your policies is up to date. This information includes your address, contact information, and any listed beneficiaries.

For example, Cedrick, a 50-year-old electrician, updated his life insurance policy to include his new spouse as a beneficiary after moving to a new home and updating his address.

Step 5: Assess Coverage for Major Life Changes

Consider any recent life changes and how they might impact your insurance needs. Adjust your coverage accordingly to ensure you are fully protected.

A 42-year-old auto mechanic, Carlos, reviewed his health insurance policy after being diagnosed with a chronic condition. He switched to a plan with better coverage for her medical needs, ensuring he received the necessary care without excessive out-of-pocket costs.

Working with an Insurance Agent

An insurance agent can be a valuable resource when reviewing and updating your policies. They can provide expert advice, help you find discounts, and ensure you have the right coverage.

A 40-year-old plumber, Jin, schedules an annual review with his insurance agent. The agent helps Jin identify gaps in his coverage and suggests policy adjustments to better protect his assets.

Questions to Ask Your Agent

When working with your insurance agent, ask the following questions to ensure you are getting the best coverage:

1. Are there any new discounts I qualify for?

2. Do I have adequate coverage for my current assets and liabilities?

3. Are there any policy riders or endorsements that would benefit me?

4. How does my deductible impact my premiums, and should I consider adjusting it?

5. Are there any changes in the insurance market that could affect my coverage or rates?

Patience, a 32-year-old architect, asks her insurance agent about potential discounts. The agent informs her about a discount for installing a home security system, which Patience takes advantage of, lowering her homeowner's insurance premium.

Using Technology to Manage Your Policies

In today's digital age, managing your insurance policies can be easier with the help of Technology. Many insurance companies offer online portals and mobile apps that allow you to review and update your policies, file claims, and access important documents.

Seth, a 38-year-old IT support manager, uses his insurance company's mobile app to review his auto insurance policy. The app allows him to update his personal information, adjust coverage limits, and file a claim if needed.

Benefits of Using Technology

Convenience: Access your policies anytime, anywhere.

Efficiency: Quickly update information and make changes.

Organization: Store and manage all your insurance documents in one place.

Notifications: Receive alerts and reminders for policy renewals and payments.

Abigail, a 45-year-old personal trainer, receives a notification on her phone reminding her that her homeowners insurance policy is up for renewal. She logs into the app, reviews her coverage, and makes necessary updates, all from the comfort of her home.

Reviewing Specific Types of Insurance

Each type of insurance has unique aspects to consider when reviewing and updating your policies. Here are some tips for specific types:

Auto Insurance

- Mileage Adjustments: If you are driving less, you might qualify for lower rates.

- Vehicle Changes: Update your policy when you buy or sell a car.

- Teen Drivers: Add young drivers to your policy and inquire about discounts for good students or safe driving courses.

Cassandra, a 35-year-old caregiver, updated her auto insurance policy to reflect her reduced mileage after starting a remote job. This change lowers her premium, saving her money each month.

Homeowners Insurance

- Home Renovations: Ensure your policy reflects any significant improvements or additions.

- Property Value: Adjust coverage based on current home value and replacement costs.

- High-Value Items: Add coverage for new high-value items such as jewelry or electronics.

Jeremiah, a 40-year-old pharmacist, is renovating his kitchen and adding a home office. He updates his homeowner's insurance policy to reflect these improvements, ensuring he has adequate coverage for the increased value of his home.

Health Insurance

- Open Enrollment: Review and update your health insurance during the annual open enrollment period.

- Changing Needs: Adjust your plan based on new medical conditions, prescriptions, or family additions.

- Preventive Care: Ensure your plan covers necessary preventive services.

A 28-year-old waitress, Clara reviews her health insurance options during open enrollment. In anticipation of starting a family, she switches to a plan with better maternity coverage.

Life Insurance

- Beneficiary Updates: Regularly update beneficiaries to reflect changes in your family situation.

- Coverage Amount: Adjust your coverage as your financial responsibilities grow or decrease.

- Policy Types: Consider converting term policies to permanent ones if your needs change.

Jude, a 38-year-old electrician, updated his life insurance policy to include his new child as a beneficiary and increased his coverage to ensure his family's financial security.

Tips for Busy Professionals and Parents

Balancing work and family and managing your insurance policies can be challenging. Here are some tips to help you stay on top of your insurance needs:

1. Schedule Regular Reviews

Set a reminder to review your insurance policies annually or after significant life events. This proactive approach ensures you stay adequately covered.

Olson, a 50-year-old attorney, sets a calendar reminder to review his insurance policies every January. This yearly habit helps him keep his coverage up to date.

2. Use a Personal Insurance Checklist

Create a checklist of all your insurance policies and review each one systematically. This organized approach ensures you notice all essential details.

Meredith, a 45-year-old marketing manager, creates a checklist with sections for auto, home, health, and life insurance. She systematically reviews each policy, making necessary updates and ensuring comprehensive coverage.

3. Work with a Trusted Agent

Develop a relationship with a dependable insurance agent who understands your needs and can provide personalized advice. Regular check-ins with your agent can help you stay on top of your insurance requirements.

Mary, a 32-year-old school superintendent, schedules an annual review with her insurance agent. The agent helps her identify new discounts, adjust coverage, and ensure her policies align with her current needs.

Regularly reviewing and updating your insurance policies is crucial to maintaining financial security and protecting your assets. By staying proactive and making necessary adjustments, you can ensure your coverage keeps pace with your life changes and evolving risks. Whether you are a busy professional, a parent, or simply someone focused on personal growth and financial well-being, these strategies will help you navigate the insurance landscape confidently and safely.

In the next chapter, we will explore the future of insurance and how emerging trends and technologies are shaping the industry. From telematics to artificial intelligence, you will learn how to leverage these innovations to your advantage and stay ahead in the ever-evolving world of insurance.

Chapter Fourteen

The Future of Insurance and Personal Finance

"Change is the law of life. And those who look only to the past or present are certain to miss the future."
– John F. Kennedy

As the world around us evolves rapidly, so does the landscape of insurance and personal finance. Emerging technologies and shifting societal trends are reshaping how we manage our financial well-being and protect ourselves from unexpected events. This chapter will explore the exciting future of insurance and personal finance, using simple and everyday examples to illustrate key concepts.

The Rise of Telematics in Auto Insurance

Telematics is revolutionizing the auto insurance industry by using technology to monitor driving behavior. This data-driven approach offers insurance companies more personalized and fair premiums based on actual driving habits rather than generalized risk factors.

Imagine you are Jisoo, a 32-year-old college professor who commutes to work every day. You enroll in a usage-based insurance program that uses a telematics device to track your driving habits, such as speed, braking, and mileage. Because you are a cautious driver, you receive a discount on your premium, saving you money each month.

Benefits of Telematics

- Personalized Premiums: Pay based on your actual driving behavior.

- Improved Safety: Monitoring can encourage safer driving habits.

- Cost Savings: Potential for significant discounts for safe drivers.

Johnson, a 40-year-old freelancer, finds his telematics program offers additional discounts for participating in safe driving challenges. He enjoys competing with himself to improve his driving scores, and the savings on his premium are a bonus.

The Impact of Artificial Intelligence (AI) on Insurance

Artificial intelligence transforms the insurance industry by enhancing underwriting, claims processing, and customer service. AI algorithms can analyze vast amounts of data to assess risk more accurately, streamline operations, and provide personalized experiences.

AI in Underwriting

AI-driven underwriting can quickly analyze various data points, such as credit scores, social media activity, and health records, to determine risk and set premiums more accurately.

Helen, a 45-year-old Software manager, applies for life insurance. Instead of waiting weeks for a decision, an AI-powered underwriting system evaluates her application in minutes, considering several factors to provide an accurate premium quote.

AI in Claims Processing

AI can expedite claims processing by automating routine tasks, detecting fraud, and making data-driven decisions.

Lee, a 50-year-old teacher, files a claim for water damage in his home. An AI system quickly reviews the photos and documents he uploads, approves the claim, and initiates payment within hours instead of days.

AI in Customer Service

AI-powered chatbots and virtual assistants can handle routine inquiries, provide policy information, and guide customers through the claims process.

Flora, a 35-year-old medical researcher, uses her insurance company's virtual assistant to update her policy information and ask about available discounts. The AI chatbot answers her questions promptly, providing a seamless customer service experience.

Blockchain Technology in Insurance

Blockchain technology offers a secure and transparent way to manage insurance contracts and transactions. It can reduce fraud, streamline claims processing, and enhance trust between insurers and policyholders.

Benefits of Blockchain

- Enhanced Security: Immutable records prevent tampering and fraud.

- Transparency: Clear and transparent transactions build trust.

- Efficiency: Automated processes reduce administrative costs and speed up claims.

A 40-year-old investment banker, Alvin purchases travel insurance using a blockchain-based platform. When his flight is delayed, the smart contract automatically triggers a payout, and the funds are transferred to his account without the need for a lengthy claims process.

The Growing Importance of Cyber Insurance

As our reliance on digital technologies increases, so does the risk of cyber-attacks. Cyber insurance is becoming essential for protecting individuals and businesses from the financial impact of data breaches, hacking, and other cyber threats.

Cecily, a 32-year-old Massage Therapist, experiences identity theft when her personal information is stolen online. Thankfully, her cyber insurance policy covers restoring her identity, including legal fees, lost wages, and credit monitoring services.

Benefits of Cyber Insurance

- Financial Protection: Covers costs associated with cyber incidents.

- Risk Mitigation: Offers resources for preventing and responding to cyber threats.

- Peace of Mind: Provides security in an increasingly digital world.

Smith, a 40-year-old entrepreneur, runs a small online business. He invests in a comprehensive cyber insurance policy covering data breaches, ransomware attacks, and business interruption to ensure his business can recover quickly from cyber incidents.

The Role of Wearable Technology in Health Insurance

Wearable Technology, such as fitness trackers and smartwatches, is changing how health insurance companies assess risk and encourage healthy behaviors. These devices can provide real-time data on physical activity, heart rate, sleep patterns, exercise, and more.

Jolie, a 45-year-old chef, wears a fitness tracker that monitors her daily steps, exercise routines, and sleep quality. Her health insurance company offers rewards and premium discounts based on her activity levels, motivating her to maintain a healthy lifestyle.

Benefits of Wearable Technology

- Personalized Health Insights: Provides real-time data on health metrics.

- Incentives for Healthy Behaviors: Rewards policyholders for maintaining healthy habits.

- Proactive Health Management: Helps prevent illnesses through early detection and intervention.

Hancock, a 50-year-old pilot, participates in his health insurance company's wellness program. The program uses data from his smartwatch to track his progress. He earns points for meeting fitness goals, which he can redeem for gift cards and premium discounts.

The Future of Personal Finance and Insurance Integration

The future of insurance and personal finance lies in seamless integration, where financial planning and insurance coverage work together to provide comprehensive protection and growth opportunities. Here is how this integration is taking shape:

Financial Wellness Programs

Insurance companies increasingly offer financial wellness programs that help policyholders manage their finances, save for the future, and reduce debt.

Melanie, a 35-year-old realtor, enrolls in her insurance company's financial wellness program. The program provides personalized advice on budgeting, retirement savings, and debt management, helping Melanie improve her financial health.

Robo-Advisors

Robo-advisors use algorithms to provide personalized investment advice and portfolio management, making financial planning more accessible and affordable.

Ryan, a 40-year-old civil engineer, uses a robo-advisor to manage his investments. The robo-advisor automatically adjusts his portfolio based on his goals and risk tolerance, ensuring his investments align with his financial plan.

Hybrid Insurance Products

Hybrid insurance products combine traditional insurance coverage with investment components, offering policyholders the benefits of both protection and growth.

Ana, a 32-year-old nurse, purchases a hybrid life insurance policy with an investment component. The policy provides financial protection for her family while also allowing her to build cash value that she can access in the future.

The Impact of Climate Change on Insurance

Climate change is reshaping the insurance industry as extreme weather events become more frequent and severe. Insurers adapt by offering new products and adjusting their risk assessments for climate-related threats.

Timothy, a 40-year-old Uber driver, lives in an area prone to hurricanes. He updates his homeowner's insurance policy to include coverage for flood damage, ensuring his home is protected against increasingly severe weather events.

Benefits of Climate Adaptation

- Enhanced Risk Assessment: Better prediction and management of climate-related risks.

- New Insurance Products: Innovative products to cover emerging threats.

- Community Resilience: Support for rebuilding and recovery efforts.

Veronica, a 45-year-old nurse practitioner, installs a solar panel system in her home. Her insurance company offers a discount for environmentally friendly home improvements, reducing her premium and encouraging sustainable practices.

Embracing a Proactive Approach to Insurance

The future of insurance is moving towards an initiative-taking approach, where insurers use data and technology to help policyholders prevent losses and manage risks more effectively.

Predictive Analytics

Insurers use predictive analytics to identify potential risks and offer personalized recommendations to policyholders.

Deon, a 50-year-old landscaper, receives a warning from his insurance company of an approaching storm. The notification includes tips on securing his home and an offer for emergency supplies, helping Deon protect his property and minimize damage.

Risk Prevention Programs

Insurance companies offer programs that help policyholders take proactive steps to reduce risks, such as home security assessments and driver safety courses.

Magdalene, a 35-year-old store clerk, participates in a home security assessment program offered by her insurance company. The assessment identifies potential vulnerabilities, and Magdalene receives a discount on her premium for implementing the recommended improvements.

Insurance Future

The future of insurance and personal finance is bright, with innovative technologies and trends transforming how we manage risk and protect our financial well-being. From telematics and AI to blockchain and wearable Technology, these advancements offer exciting opportunities to maximize benefits, reduce costs, and enhance security.

By integrating these innovations into your financial planning, you can achieve personal growth, resilience, and peace of mind in an ever-changing world with insurance.

To wrap up our journey through insurance and personal finance, this final chapter summarizes vital takeaways and provides actionable steps to help you implement the strategies discussed throughout this guide.

Whether you are just starting your financial journey or looking to optimize your current plan, this final chapter empowers you to take control of your financial future with confidence and clarity.

Recap of Key Points

- Chapter 1: We started with the basics, demystifying insurance and highlighting its importance in safeguarding your financial future.

- Chapter 2: You learned how to assess your insurance needs based on your unique circumstances and life stages.

- Chapter 3: We dove into life insurance, helping you choose the right policy to protect your loved ones.

- Chapter 4: Health insurance complexities were broken down, ensuring you can navigate your options confidently.

- Chapter 5: We covered the essentials of auto and home insurance, emphasizing the importance of adequate coverage for your assets.

- Chapter 6: Disability and long-term care insurance were discussed, highlighting their role in comprehensive financial planning.

- Chapter 7: Delve into renter's and landlord's insurance protection against property damages.

- Chapter 8: Addressed the complexities of Medicare plans

- Chapter 9: We explored strategies for maximizing benefits while minimizing costs, helping you get the most out of your policies.

- Chapter 10: Filing claims and avoiding pitfalls were tackled, providing you with the knowledge to manage claims effectively.

- Chapter 11: Regularly reviewing and updating your policies was emphasized to keep your coverage current and adequate.

- Chapter 12: We looked at the future of insurance, including emerging trends and technologies that will shape the industry.

Taking proactive steps to manage your insurance can seem daunting, but it's essential for financial security. Review your policies regularly, update them as your life changes, and stay informed about new trends and options in the insurance industry.

Final Thoughts on Achieving Financial Security

Achieving financial security through intelligent insurance choices is not just about having the right policies but also understanding and actively managing them. Here are a few sage pieces of advice to help you on your journey:

- Stay Informed: The insurance industry is constantly evolving. Stay updated with new products and trends to ensure you get the best coverage.

- Ask Questions: Never hesitate to ask your insurance agent or provider for clarification on policy details or coverage options.

- Document Everything: Keep detailed records of your policies, claims, and communications. This record will make the process smoother and less stressful if you need to file a claim.

- Hold Regular Policy Reviews with Your Agent: Schedule annual reviews of all your insurance policies to make sure they meet your needs and adjust as needed.

Remember, insurance is a crucial part of your overall financial strategy. It is your safety net, providing protection and peace of mind so you can focus on achieving your goals and enjoying life. By taking the time to understand your needs, choosing the right policies, and managing them proactively, you are setting yourself up for a secure and prosperous future.

So, this is how to make insurance work for you. May your financial journey be smooth, your risks well-managed, and your peace of mind unwavering. In memory of you, pick a copy of this book as a gift to someone you love. Cheers to a well-protected and financially secure future!

Book- End Review

Make a Lasting Impact with Your Review

"The essence of strategy is choosing what not to do."
Michael Porter

The Ripple Effect of Generosity

There's something powerful about sharing your knowledge, your experiences, and even your feedback. It not only helps others, but enriches your journey. And you can make that impact right now.

Let me ask you...

Would you take a moment to help someone you've never met, even if you receive nothing in return?

Who is this person, you ask? They're like you—busy juggling many responsibilities and trying to make the best financial decisions for themselves and their loved ones. They need a guide, a clear path to navigate the often confusing world of insurance.

This is where *How to Make Insurance Work for You: A Personal Finance Guide* comes in. My mission is to make this guide accessible to everyone who needs it. But to do that, I need your help.

Here's where you come in. People often decide whether to pick up a book based on its reviews. So, I'm asking you, on behalf of that busy professional, parent, or self-improvement enthusiast who's looking for answers:

Please take a moment to leave a review for this book.

Your review won't cost you anything; it only takes about 60 seconds. But those 60 seconds can make a world of difference for someone else. Your review could help...

...one more family makes smarter financial choices.

...one more person gains the peace of mind they've been searching for.

...one more reader finds the guidance they need to secure their future.

To create that ripple effect of generosity and help someone on their journey, all you need to do is...

Please scan the QR code or click the link below to leave your review.

https://www.amazon.com/review/review-your-purchases/?asin=B0DFFV 4TDS

If you feel good about helping a faceless single mom or dad, a newlywed or divorced, a young graduate, a busy professional, or a retiree, you are my kind of person. Welcome to the club. You're one of us.

Thank you from the bottom of my heart.

- Your biggest fan,

David Okonah

P.S. - Fun fact: When you provide something of value to another person, it makes you more valuable to them. If you believe this book will help another family member, friend, or someone important to you, consider sending it their way. Your act of kindness could make a real difference in their journey to insurance literacy and financial security.

Appendices

This section is a handy reference for all the key concepts, terms, and tools discussed throughout the book. Whether reviewing your policies or shopping for new insurance, these resources will help you stay informed and organized.

Glossary of Insurance Terms

Understanding insurance jargon can be half the battle. Here is a glossary of terms to help you navigate the world of insurance with ease:

Policy: The official document that explains what your insurance covers.

Premium: The amount you pay for your insurance policy, typically monthly, quarterly, or annually.

Copayment (Copay): A small, fixed amount you pay when you get a service covered by your insurance, like a doctor's visit.

Coinsurance: A percentage of the cost you must pay after paying your deductible.

Insurer: A company or organization that provides insurance coverage to individuals or entities.

Claim: When you ask your insurance to pay for something, they agreed to cover in the policy.

Grace Period: Extra time you get to pay your premium without losing your insurance.

Final Expense Insurance: A type of life insurance specifically designed to cover the costs associated with an individual's funeral, burial, and other end-of-life expenses.

Deductible: The amount you must pay out-of-pocket before your insurance coverage kicks in.

Liability Coverage: Protects you from economic loss if you are found legally responsible for someone else's injury or property damage.

Policy Limit: The maximum amount your insurance company will pay for a covered loss.

Rider: An add-on to an insurance policy providing coverage for specific risks or items.

Adjuster: A person who looks at the damage and decides how much the insurance should pay.

Claim: A payment request based on the terms of your insurance policy.

Payout: The money the insurance company gives you when you make a claim.

Term Insurance: Insurance that lasts for a set number of years, like 10 or 20 years.

Endorsement: A change or addition to your insurance policy that adjusts the coverage.

Claimant: The person who makes a claim to get paid by the insurance.

Third-Party Insurance: Insurance that covers damage or injury you cause to someone else.

Depreciation: The reduction in the value of something over time, which can affect how much insurance pays.

Indemnity: A promise that the insurance will pay for your loss and make you financially whole again.

Whole Life Insurance: Insurance that lasts your entire life as long as you keep paying for it.

Adjuster: An insurance company representative assesses the damage and determines the claim payment amount.

Exclusion: Specific conditions or circumstances not covered by the insurance policy.

Replacement Cost: The amount it costs to replace something with a new one, which insurance can help pay.

Excess: Another term for deductible, which is the amount you pay before insurance helps.

Annuity: A type of insurance that pays you a regular income for life or a set period.

Beneficiary: The person or entity designated to receive the benefits from an insurance policy.

Subrogation: When your insurance company gets back money from the person or company that caused the loss after they pay your claim.

Underwriting: The process by which an insurance company evaluates the risk of insuring a person or asset and sets the policy terms and premiums.

Useful Resources and Links

General Insurance Resources

- **Insurance Information Institute**
  www.iii.org
  Provides comprehensive information on various types of insurance and industry updates.

  National Association of Insurance Commissioners (NAIC)
  www.naic.org
  Offers resources to understand state-specific insurance regulations and consumer protection information.

  Health Insurance Resources

- **Healthcare.gov**
  www.healthcare.gov
  A federal government site with information on health insurance, including the Health Insurance Marketplace.

  Medicare
  www.medicare.gov

- **Centers for Medicare & Medicaid Services (CMS)**
  www.cms.gov

- **National Council on Aging**
  www.ncoa.org

Social Security and Financial Well-being

- **Social Security Administration (SSA)**
  www.ssa.gov

- **AnnualCreditReport.com**
  www.annualcreditreport.com
  Access your free annual credit report to check for accuracy and understand how your credit impacts your insurance premiums.

Consumer Resources

- **Consumer Reports**
  www.consumerreports.org
  Offers reviews and ratings for insurance companies and policies.

Chapter Fifteen

References

Buffett, W. (n.d.). *Berkshire Hathaway annual shareholder letters*. Retrieved from https://www.berkshirehathaway.com/letters/letters.html

Drucker, P. (1967). *The effective executive*. New York, NY: Harper & Row.

Franklin, B. (1758). *The way to wealth*. Philadelphia, PA: The Pennsylvania Gazette.

Franklin, B. (1784). *Franklin's letters to young people on education*. Philadelphia, PA: Publisher Not Identified.

Gandhi, M. (n.d.). The best way to find yourself is to lose yourself in the service of others [Quote]. Retrieved from https://www.goodreads.com/quotes

Kennedy, J. F. (1963, June 25). *Address in the Assembly Hall at the Paulskirche in Frankfurt*. American Presidency Project. Retrieved from https://www.presidency.ucsb.edu/node/236211

Kiyosaki, R. T. (1997). *Rich dad poor dad: What the rich teach their kids about money that the poor and middle class do not!*. Scottsdale, AZ: Plata Publishing.

Lakein, A. (1973). *How to get control of your time and your life*. New York, NY: New American Library.

Malcolm X. (1965). *Malcolm X speaks: Selected speeches and statements* (G. Breitman, Ed.). New York, NY: Grove Press.